INSIDE THE
SIMPLE LIFE

"*Inside the Simple Life* reveals a fascinating, firsthand look at a conservative Amish community that is seldom noticed. Author Susan Hougelman works among the New Wilmington Amish in western Pennsylvania. In her book, she shares winsome stories, helpful information, and stunning photographs of how her Amish neighbors live a Plain life in an increasingly complicated world."

—**SUZANNE WOODS FISHER**, bestselling author of *Anna's Crossing*, a novel about the first Amish who came to America

"Susan Hougelman does an outstanding job describing the deeply rooted and treasured values of Amish culture and her beloved community in New Wilmington, Pennsylvania. The stories of Susan's personal interactions with the Amish in New Wilmington are very real and moving. Again and again, I found myself feeling challenged and motivated to slow down and smell the roses, live a simpler life, and make my family and community a much higher priority."

—**JOE KEIM**, author of *My People, the Amish*

"Susan Hougelman has an inside view of the Amish in our area, as she is considered their friend. I live in the area, and I was pleased to take her Amish tour several years ago. She shared her knowledge and friendship about each family as we drove in and around the community. She is a gifted storyteller, and *Inside the Simple Life* is a delightful journey to take with her. You will enjoy meeting the Amish community of western Pennsylvania."

—**SANDRA JOSEPH**, biblical life coach, speaker, and blogger

"*Inside the Simple Life* by Susan Hougelman is a beautiful portrait of the Amish community and a reminder of what's most important in life—faith, family, and slowing down to appreciate God's beauty. Her delightful stories of her adventures with her Amish friends are heartfelt, insightful, hilarious, and inspirational. Readers will enjoy this special peek into the Plain life as well as the breathtaking photographs that will inspire them to pack their suitcases and experience Amish country for themselves."

—AMY CLIPSTON, bestselling author of *The Jam and Jelly Nook*

"In these pages, Susan Hougelman brings you into the world and lives of her Amish friends. You will learn about Amish ways and the rhythms of life in one of the country's oldest Amish communities. You will also be inspired. What a neat book!"

—ERIK WESNER, founder of Amish America website and YouTube channel

INSIDE THE
SIMPLE LIFE

Finding Inspiration among the Amish

SUSAN HOUGELMAN

HERALD
P R E S S

Harrisonburg, Virginia

Herald Press
PO Box 866, Harrisonburg, Virginia 22803
www.HeraldPress.com

Library of Congress Cataloging-in-Publication Data
Names: Hougelman, Susan, author.
Title: Inside the simple life : finding inspiration among the Amish / by Susan Hougelman.
Other titles: Finding inspiration among the Amish
Description: Harrisonburg, Virginia : Herald Press, [2021]
Identifiers: LCCN 2021032582 (print) | LCCN 2021032583 (ebook) | ISBN
    9781513809489 (hardback) | ISBN 9781513809496 (ebook)
Subjects: LCSH: Amish—United States—Social life and customs. | Amish—United States—
    Pictorial works. | Simplicity—Religious aspects—Amish. | BISAC: RELIGION /
    Christianity / Amish | TRAVEL / Special Interest / Religious
Classification: LCC E184.M45 H68 2021 (print) | LCC E184.M45 (ebook) |
    DDC 289.7/30973—dc23
LC record available at https://lccn.loc.gov/2021032582
LC ebook record available at https://lccn.loc.gov/2021032583

Study guides are available for many Herald Press titles at www.HeraldPress.com.

INSIDE THE SIMPLE LIFE
© 2021 by Herald Press, Harrisonburg, Virginia 22803. 800-245-7894.
    All rights reserved.
Library of Congress Control Number: 2021032582
International Standard Book Number: 978-1-5138-0948-9 (hardcover)
Printed in United States of America
Cover photo by Grant Beachy
Unless otherwise indicated, photographs by Jim Fisher, used with permission of the photographer
Cover and interior design by Merrill Miller

Scripture quotations, unless otherwise indicated, are taken from the *Holy Bible, New International Version*®, NIV®. Copyright ©1973, 1978, 1984, 2011 by Biblica, Inc.™ Used by permission of Zondervan. All rights reserved worldwide. www.zondervan.com. The "NIV" and "New International Version" are trademarks registered in the United States Patent and Trademark Office by Biblica, Inc.™

Scripture quotations marked (NLT) are taken from the *Holy Bible, New Living Translation*, copyright ©1996, 2004, 2015 by Tyndale House Foundation. Used by permission of Tyndale House Publishers, Inc., Carol Stream, Illinois 60188. All rights reserved.

Scripture quotations marked (KJV) are taken from the *Holy Bible, King James Version*.

25 24 23 22   10 9 8 7 6 5 4 3 2

This book is dedicated first and foremost to Jesus Christ my Savior, through whom all blessings flow. May he receive the glory and honor, and may this book always point people to him.

It is also dedicated to the love of my life, Joseph Edward Hougelman, my two beautiful and talented daughters, Alexandra and Lauren, and my Amish community in New Wilmington, Pennsylvania, whom I love dearly.

I pray that this book brings blessings to all who read it.

CONTENTS

"Therefore do not worry about tomorrow, for tomorrow will worry about itself. Each day has enough trouble of its own."
—Matthew 6:34

INTRODUCTION

NEW WILMINGTON is a little borough nestled in the rolling hills of western Pennsylvania. Located in Lawrence County, New Wilmington is about sixty miles north of Pittsburgh. We are a small town with a big heart, filled with about twenty-five hundred residents, including farmers, professors, students, small business owners, and hard workers. We are also home to what I believe to be the greatest Amish community in the world. The members of the Old Order Amish community surrounding New Wilmington call themselves the Lawrence County Amish, or the Byler settlement.

The first Amish families migrated to the New Wilmington area in about 1845 and just five years later, in 1850, organized their first church. There were about twenty-five families in the first Amish church district, and from those families, two ordained ministers and a bishop.

Today there are (more or less) 2,388 Amish people, 604 families, 300 young folks, 515 schoolchildren, twenty schools, and one special "sunbeam" school (for children with mental handicaps) within the Lawrence County Amish community. Most of the Amish families are named Byler, hence "the Byler settlement." But there are also Hostetlers, Kempfs, Kurtzes, Lees, Masts, Millers, Shetlers, Swartzentrubers, Troyers, Wengerds, Yoders, and a Detweiler.

I have fallen in love with the Amish community of Lawrence County. I have been invited into their lives as a friend, and many have become like family to me, even though I am an English person (what the Amish call non-Amish people). I have been a guest at Amish weddings and a mourner at funerals. I have had dinners with Amish families in their homes and they have had dinner in mine. We have shopped together, celebrated holidays together, and traveled on vacation together. I have made apple butter with four generations of Amish women, and I have watched them quilt and sew and do laundry. I have helped bring families together. I've been invited into one-room Amish schoolhouses to watch the children perform in their Christmas programs, and I got to examine their textbooks and schoolbooks. I have driven Amish friends to hospitals to have babies and to bring those babies home. I held the hand of a young Amish mother after her baby was stillborn and held another Amish woman in my arms as she sobbed after losing her son in a farming accident. I know all their children's names as well as the names of their pets. God has helped create a beautiful relationship and bond between myself and the Amish people that continues to grow with each passing year. (Throughout this book, I have changed individuals' names to protect their privacy.)

How my relationship with the Amish community began

I began my career in New Wilmington as the proprietor of our family restaurant, the Tavern on the Square. When my husband Joe and I

first opened our restaurant, I was the greeter for people as they walked through the front door, and I began to notice something rather unusual—people would often come to my host station and ask me where they could go and see the Amish. You see, the New Wilmington area had a very nice-sized Amish population, but there was no tourism centered around the Amish community. The Amish lived and worked here in New Wilmington, but they pretty much kept to themselves. There was an Amish-owned quilt shop that was open to the public, and several produce stands, but other than that, I didn't know there were other shops or places for folks to visit. So when people would ask, "Where can we see the Amish?" I would tell them, "You just have to drive around and look for them."

I must make a confession. Even though I had grown up in New Wilmington and lived here most of my life, I had never really talked to an Amish person. That seems so strange now, but the truth is that

Our beloved Tavern Restaurant located in the heart of Amish Country. I brought many Amish families here. For some Amish children it was their first time in a restaurant. PHOTO BY SUSAN HOUGELMAN

English and Amish people didn't mix much except to do business with each other. My parents lived across the street from an Amish family and I would say hello and wave when they were outside, and we did have an Amish man make the dining room furniture for the Tavern, but other than that, the Amish were just a part of life in New Wilmington that most of us viewed from afar. It was normal for us to pass a horse and buggy on the road, and to see people dressed in blue wearing bonnets and hats, but it would have been uncommon to have these folks as friends.

One day, someone came to the Tavern and asked, "Excuse me, ma'am, where can we go to see the Amish?" But this time, instead of telling them to drive around, I said, "Would you like me to show you where the Amish are?" That's how I started Simple Life Tours. Okay, so that's not exactly how it happened. Remember, I had never really had a conversation with an Amish person before. I had very little knowledge about where they lived, and I didn't even know if I was permitted to

I was sitting at a table inside of my restaurant when I snapped this photo. God gave me a glimpse of my future that day. PHOTO BY SUSAN HOUGELMAN

enter their world, let alone bring other people into it. But I saw a need that wasn't being met and I saw an opportunity. I felt God's call on my life, and I knew that he was leading me down a new path. This time God was calling me toward the Amish people.

Simple Life Tours and getting to know the Amish

If I was going to teach people about the Amish and take them on tours to see the Amish, I was probably going to have to learn all I could about the Amish people and their way of life. So I began to research and read everything I could find about the Amish. I had no idea they came from Switzerland! (I thought it was Germany.) I didn't know they weren't allowed to use tractors for farming. (In our Amish community they are allowed to farm with only horse, hand, and plow.) I didn't know where they went to school, or where their churches were. I didn't even know that Amish was a way of life and not their religion. What was their religion?

Oh, I had so much to learn. The more I read, the more I began to admire the Amish way of life. I would often find myself saying, "That's how it should be . . . I wish life were like that for all of us . . . That's how we should do church." God began to draw my heart toward this fascinating group of people, and I wanted to get to know them in person, not just by what I read on the Internet.

I enlisted a friend to help. Audrene Burns is a beautiful Christ follower, fellow entrepreneur, and good friend. Audrene owns an Angus beef farm. Not only does she do business with our local Amish community, but she also lives among them. If anyone would know about the Amish, she would. I called Audrene on a Tuesday afternoon and asked her if she would take me to every Amish business that she knew existed here in the New Wilmington area and introduce me to her Amish friends. That Saturday, Audrene picked me up in her mud-covered truck (farm life!) and handed me a hand-drawn map. On the back of

the map was a list of ten Amish-owned businesses that she thought I would like to see. She wrote down the name of each business, their address, and the names of the Amish business owners. (I will always be grateful to Audrene for helping me get started.)

Our very first stop was a grocery store located in the basement of an Amish home. Although it was on the same road where my parents owned a home, I had no idea this grocery store existed. We pulled up next to a horse and buggy tied up to a hitching post. Audrene said, "That's the Amish parking lot. Never park your car in front of it. The horse and buggies will have nowhere to park when they visit the store." I took out my notebook and wrote down, *Don't park in front of any hitching posts.* "Got it!" I replied.

Audrene walked ahead of me. I must admit I was a bit nervous. Was I allowed to make eye contact with them? Could I shake their hand? Did they speak our language? Would they say no if I asked whether I could bring people to see their business? Maybe they would even shun me if they knew I was starting a tour company. Audrene opened the door, and my eyes were immediately drawn toward the oil lamp that hung from a hook in the ceiling. I had wondered how they lit their homes with no electricity. They used oil lamps! There was a young Amish mother standing behind a small counter with the cutest little boy sitting on a large chest freezer. He looked to be about four years old.

"Hello," I said with a smile. "How are you today?"

"Susan," Audrene said with a giggle, "he doesn't speak English. The Amish speak a language called Pennsylvania Dutch. They don't learn English until they go to school."

Oh, I felt so silly. I shrugged my shoulders and smiled awkwardly. "Audrene," I whispered, "how do they use a freezer with no electricity?"

"That's an icebox," she replied. "They don't plug it in. They get fifty-pound blocks of ice delivered from an iceman. They put those blocks of ice in the chest freezer, and that acts as their refrigerator. It will keep items cold for a week." Again, I had no idea. I felt as if I were in a foreign country.

Audrene then introduced me to the sweet Amish woman behind the counter. She was wearing a blue dress, and her hair was tucked under a white bonnet, which the Amish call a *Kapp*. "Susan Hougelman, this is Anna Byler and her son Aaron. Anna Byler, this is Susan Hougelman. She owns the Tavern on the Square restaurant."

"Nice to meet you," I said. "Have you ever been to the Tavern?"

"No," Anna replied, "I have not."

Oh brother! That was probably another stupid question. After all, I had never seen an Amish person in our restaurant. Embarrassed, I walked away from the counter and began to look around the little store. There were three long rows of shelves, and each shelf was packed full. I saw giant bags of flour, sugar, and rice. There were pastas, soup mixes, beans, and cereals. I saw homemade jams and jellies, peanut butter, local honey, and lots of candy and snack foods. When I looked at the prices of these items, I couldn't believe my eyes. They were very low compared to our local grocery stores. "Yes," I told Audrene, "I most certainly want to bring my guests here to this store."

I walked back up to the counter and said, "Anna, I really like your store. Would you mind if I brought other people to see your store?" She smiled so sweetly and replied in a soft voice, "No, I wouldn't mind."

And that's how Simple Life Tours was born.

I've been taking people to see the beautiful Amish countryside of New Wilmington for seven years now. In the time since I started Simple Life Tours in 2013, we have sold our restaurant and I now tour full-time. I never dreamed that this would be the career path that the Lord would take me on, and I never imagined how the Amish people and their way of life would change my own life.

At first, my encounters with the Amish business owners were brief and simple. I would say hello and smile when I entered the business, and "Thank you for letting us visit" when I left. My tours were infrequent, maybe three or four a month, but as my business started to grow, I started taking two or three trips a week to see the Amish, and

PHOTOS BY SUSAN HOUGELMAN

eventually they became daily adventures. Sometimes I had four or five tours per day.

To get to know the families on my tour stops on a deeper, more personal level, I began inviting them to dinner at my restaurant. Owning a restaurant was a great blessing for me in developing closer relationships to the Amish people. In our community, the members of the Old Order Amish are not supposed to sit down in a restaurant unless they are invited by an "Englisher." My friend Gideon shared with me that his bishop says it is shameful to waste money in a restaurant when there are people in China without Bibles. That money they would spend eating out could serve a much greater purpose. (This was the first lesson I learned from my Amish friends.)

I would invite them for meals at the Tavern, and we would share stories about our lives. They would graciously answer any questions I had about the Amish culture, but mostly we were just friends sharing a meal together and enjoying each other's company.

There are two conversations from those early dinners that stand out most. One is when I asked an Amish woman if they ever get asked funny questions by English people. My friend Anna answered, "My favorite question is, 'What's it like to be Amish?' I say, 'I don't know any different! What's it like to be English?'"

To Anna, that was such a strange question. She went on to say that the Amish are people like everyone else. "We dress differently and live a little differently from English people, but inside we're the same as you." That helped me learn early on to treat the Amish people as I would any other human beings, with love, kindness, and respect.

The second conversation was one of the first times I invited Amish women—three sisters and their mother—to lunch at the Tavern. I was nervous. This was in the beginning of my getting to know Amish people, and I still didn't know whether there were boundaries; if there were, I surely didn't want to cross them! After enjoying a delicious meal of chicken and biscuits, with homemade coconut cream pie for dessert, I asked the women if they would mind if I asked them some questions.

"No, Susan, we don't mind. Ask us anything."

The very first question I had for them was, "Is there a reason why you push your curtains to the side?" Most of the Amish in our community have white curtains that are pulled to one side of the window. I heard that it meant that a young woman who lives there is available to marry, and I wanted to know if that was true.

Two of the sisters looked at me, smiled, and said, "Susan, there's no reason. That's just the way we hang them." The third sister giggled.

From their reactions and the looks on their faces, I thought that they had a secret, and they weren't going to share it with me. I was disappointed. I'd heard that the Amish were very private, but I didn't think that this was something they would want to keep hidden.

That third sister who giggled looked at me and said, "Oh yes, there's a reason we hang them that way!" The other sisters and their mom sort of gave her the stink eye, and this got my heart beating a little bit faster. *Yes, she was going to tell me the secret!* She said, "Susan, come closer and I'll whisper it to you."

Oh my goodness, it was so secretive that she had to whisper it to me! My heart was really racing now! I leaned in, and she said, rather loudly, "We Amish hang our curtains to the side because it lets the light in! We have no electricity, dummy!"

All four of them broke out in laughter as I covered my eyes with my hand and groaned. I learned two lessons that day. One, that curtains pushed to the side does not mean there's an available daughter at home, and two, that the Amish love to laugh and have great senses of humor!

The more I toured, and the more I visited Amish friends, the more I began to see how different their lives were from my own and that of most other "English" families I knew. Our world seems to buzz by

Sometimes people call the Amish in Lawrence County "the blue door Amish" because most of the houses have blue doors. There's an old wives' tale that it means a young unmarried woman is available, but that's simply not true.

so swiftly, like a subway train zooming full speed down the tracks, while the Amish live life at a much slower pace. (Like an Amish buggy clip-clopping along a country road, as if the people inside were just driving out and about and enjoying the scenery.) I used to think that success meant having a lot of money, a big house, and a fancy car—until my Amish friends taught me a different definition of success. The Amish value God, family, and community as much higher priorities than making money, going on vacations, or having nice things, as we tend to do. We say God and family are most important to us, but our actions don't always prove that.

The more I learned, the more I realized that many of us are seeking a different way to live life, too. We all want to live in a place that treasures truth, good values, and family and community. I have found that place among the Amish.

Getting to know the Amish and their way of life has changed my life. In this fast-paced and ever-changing world full of chaos and uncertainty, I have been transformed by the steadfast truth, godly values, and biblical principles as I have seen them lived out among the Amish. They have shown me that it's possible for a community to exist where peace and tranquility flourish, where "Love thy neighbor" means more than just a wave or a friendly greeting. The Amish put love into action! I have found a place where all needs, physical and emotional, are taken care of by members of the community. I have learned how to slow down and enjoy life. I've learned how to live a simpler life and have found great inspiration among the Amish people. It's my greatest honor to be able to share these stories with you, and I hope they inspire you as much as they have me.

"Love the Lord your God with all your heart and with all your soul and with all your mind and with all your strength.' The second is this: 'Love your neighbor as yourself.' There is no commandment greater than these."—Mark 12:30-31

"I have told you these things, so that in me you may have peace. In this world you will have trouble. But take heart! I have overcome the world." —John 16:33

"Thy word is a lamp unto my feet, and a light unto my path."
—Psalm 119:105 KJV

*"For where two or three are gathered together in my name,
there am I in the midst of them."—Matthew 18:20 KJV*

ONE

GOD AND CHURCH

THE AMISH don't just go to church, they *are* the church.

Have you ever heard the phrase "Don't go to church, be the church"? Too often, we have a consumer mindset about church. We go, listen to some great worship music, visit with some friends, hear a sermon, and go home. Many of us shop around and try to find a church that we like on the basis of its music, or sermon style, or what kind of building it is housed in. But, friends, I've learned that church isn't a building, and we are not consumers. We are the church. We are God's hands and feet here on earth, and we are chosen by God to be those hands and feet to meet one another's needs. By actively *being* the church, we are fulfilling God's greatest commandment: to love one another!

Nobody demonstrates that more than the Amish.

The Amish do not attend church in a typical church building; rather, they hold worship services in their own homes. There is no "church hopping" from church to church. Services are held every other Sunday. The off Sundays are called "visiting Sundays," when the Amish are permitted to visit other church districts, but most of my Amish friends take the day to rest.

The Amish in Lawrence County are broken up into geographic districts. There are about twenty districts here, and each is its own church district. There are about twenty-five families in each church district, totaling approximately 100–125 people, including men, women, and children.

I was privileged to host a group of little Amish girls at my home for a day of fun before they went back to school. It was the first time these girls were in an English home, so you can imagine how much fun they had using the bathroom, making ice come out of the refrigerator door, seeing a dishwasher and an iron, and even seeing hot water come from a faucet . . . things we so often take for granted.

I must share with you the sweetest part of the day. The girls had each brought their Amish dolls (little cloth dolls with no faces), which were wearing either a white or black cap. Some dolls had blue scarves, some had black capes and black Amish girls' socks, and others were wrapped in baby blankets with a binkie attached to a piece of yarn hung around their neck. Each girl also had a little train traveling case, which is what Amish women use for diaper bags. And those cases were filled with Amish toys and books and little diapers and pretend bottles for the babies. I had my own baby doll (that I use for decoration in my Amish-themed room), and they brought me a blanket for my "baby."

The girls wanted to play "church," so they lined up my ottomans and chairs to be the church benches. Amish women line up for church, from oldest to youngest, in the basement of the home hosting that week's service, and Amish men usually line up in the barn. I asked the

An Amish doll with a copy of the Ausbund. PHOTO BY SUSAN HOUGELMAN, USED WITH PERMISSION.

The church bench wagon on its way to the next meeting location.

A Sunday walk to church

girls how they knew who was oldest, next oldest, and so on, and they said, "We just know from doing it so many times." I had forgotten that it's the same families who attend church services together week after week, so they had done this every other Sunday for their entire lives. They had the order down pat! They added, "Men sit on the right, closest to the living room, and women sit on the left, closest to the kitchen."

So we lined up, and of course I was the oldest, but I got to go second so the oldest girl could show me what to do. You walk around the entire room, and that is exactly what each girl did, very quietly (they took it very seriously), and then we sat down in our seat. But before you sit down, you shake hands with whoever is already seated. They shook hands and nodded to each churchgoer (again, they were so serious, just like little adults), and carrying their babies and train cases, all the girls sat down. Then they began singing a German hymn, and while they sang, one girl would make a "baby crying" sound, and quietly get up with her baby and take it to the bedroom. There she would lay it down on the bed and come back and sit down. One of the girls would pretend her baby was naughty, and she would pat it on the mouth and say, "Shh."

I was in awe. I felt as though I got to be part of a secret world. The children were showing me the way they worship, and it was so lovely. During Amish church services, the babies who are old enough to eat solid food can have little pieces of moon pie (a hand pie filled with dried apples and sugar boiled down to resemble apple butter), so we had goldfish crackers to represent the moon pies. These girls were the sweetest mothers, and I could see their future in their eyes, and hearts, and actions.

Thank you, Lord, for allowing me the gift of getting to show these children your love, and for showing me *your* love through these children. I am so filled with awe and gratitude for your grace and love.

Worshiping together

The older church members sit in front. (Of course they do! They probably have trouble hearing. It would make sense for them to sit up front.) The youngest sit in front as well. (That makes sense too. They probably have a harder time paying attention and are fidgety.) Men and women sit separately so they are not distracted. I love how the Amish shake hands and look in the eye every member who has sat before them. This way, everybody gets a physical touch. If you were a lonely widow or widower, imagine how lovely it would feel to be greeted and touched by every adult and child in your church. It's a way of saying, "We care about you. You are valued." And it helps everyone to know each other. The children in every Amish church can name every person in their church, where they live, where they line up and sit. Could yours?

Church districts are smaller communities within the larger community. My Amish friend Nancy explained to me that the members of a church district become more than just neighbors—they are more like extended family members. She said, "When we have a wedding, our church family members are going to help us cook and serve the wedding meal. When there is a funeral, our church family will help make the coffin and dig the grave for our loved one. We will help pay each other's medical bills if the need arises. Susan, nobody is ever alone in the Amish community. Your church family surrounds you with love and help."

The Amish in our community are not allowed musical instruments, but they sure do sing. They normally sing three hymns per church service. Each song comes from their hymnal, the *Ausbund*, which is one of the oldest hymnals still in use in the world today. The hymns were composed during the 1500s, when the Anabaptists were being martyred. My Amish friend Andy told me that the second song that is sung in every Amish church is the same: "Das Loblied," which means a song of love and praise. He said, "Susan, every Amish person is singing this song about the same time in every single Amish church in America. This gives all of our

PHOTO BY JFLETCH/GETTY

people a sense of unity, and we know that we are all praising God at the very same time." Imagine if every single Christ follower sang the same song praising God at the same time every single Sunday. What beautiful incense that would be sent up to heaven, and how amazing it would be to know that you were a part of one body praising the Lord all together.

My favorite time to take a drive through the back roads of Amish country is on a Sunday morning at about eight-thirty. You will see families dressed in their Sunday best, walking together. You will see fathers holding their little girls' hands, brothers and sisters running ahead. Imagine if you were able to walk to church together as a family, breathing in that fresh air, passing your neighbors who are also walking to church together. A time to talk about what's going on in your life, the neighborhood, and the world.

I think it would be incredible to have a church in every neighborhood, or rather, like the Amish, to have every neighborhood be a church. Worshiping the Lord in song (everyone sings; it is not about being entertained), reading Scripture aloud, listening to a sermon, then having a meal together, where everybody helps serve and clean up. Like the Amish, I think we should close all businesses except essential ones on Sundays so most people can take a day of rest. Families would be able to stay at home and relax, or play games together, or visit with other family members or friends.

We need a day of rest. Ask any doctor and they will tell you our bodies need rest to recharge. Ask any athlete and they will tell you rest is essential to rebuild muscles. Psychologists will tell you rest is essential for the mind, and religious leaders will tell you rest is essential for the soul, and most importantly, God ordained that we rest. If you drive through Amish country, you will see many signs that say "No Sunday Sales." The Amish know that day of rest is invaluable.

Buggies gathered at a home where a group of Amish women are making moon pies for Sunday church.

Sunday preparations

My Amish friend Sarah had church at her home one week. Sarah had cleaned her home for about five weeks straight to prepare it for the church service! She had washed every linen in the entire house (remember, that is handwashed or the old Maytag wringer–washed) and hung them out to dry, even in the frigid temperatures. She had made new curtains for the entire first floor, varnished cupboards and floors, and cleaned every nook and cranny inside the house, barn, shop, and outside.

The Amish believe in giving their very best to God and their community. My Amish friend says, "Oh, if you would find dust in an Amish woman's home, she would be thought of as lazy, and *no* Amish woman wants to be thought of as lazy!" They not only clean their houses but wear their very best clothes and wash their buggies every Saturday so they are sparkling, too!

On the Saturday before church, several women from Sarah's church district came over and helped bake apple pies for the church meal after the service. These little pies are called moon pies because they are shaped like a half moon. They are made with dried apples, cinnamon, and sugar. Sometimes the women will prepare them with rhubarb, and then they are called schnitz pies. They will also serve bean soup, pickles, and homemade bread. The same meal is served after every church service so there is no competition among the women. It is also a frugal meal, so whether you are rich or poor, you can afford to feed your entire congregation. We could learn so much from our Amish friends.

The Amish bishop

In every Amish church there are deacons, ministers, and a bishop. The bishop is the head of his church district. He's the man in charge of disciplining, baptizing new members, and performing marriage ceremonies. A bishop is not a paid position—he must still have a job outside of being bishop.

I asked my friend Jake how bishops are chosen. He said, "Each Amish man makes a vow when they are baptized that they will accept the responsibility of being a deacon, minister, or bishop if chosen. When a position in the church needs filled, all the members of the church will nominate someone whom they think would make a good person to fulfill that role."

"Do women nominate this person too, or just men?" I asked.

"Women get to nominate too," answered Jake. He continued, "We take the men who had the most votes and put them in a room, where they are asked to pray. In the next room, we place a circle of chairs, as many as there are men who were selected. On each of those chairs we place a Bible, and in one of those Bibles we put a prayer card. The men are asked to prayerfully come and sit down. They each pick up a Bible, and at the same time they all open their Bibles. The man who has the prayer card tucked inside his Bible is the new bishop."

I was in awe. "It's like drawing lots in the Bible, Jake. That's how the early believers chose the disciple to replace Judas!" I can't think of any other church that chooses a leader by drawing lots, but that is straight out of the Bible!

"We feel that God chose that man to be bishop," he said.

"Jake, if God chooses someone to be bishop, does that make that man feel special or above everyone else?" I asked. "Because I think if God chose me to be the leader of my community, I would feel somewhat important."

Jake shook his head and he laughed out loud. "Oh, Susan," he said, "it's the exact opposite. When those men are praying in that room before they sit down, they are praying *not* to be bishop. Nobody wants to be the bishop! It's a hard job and a heavy responsibility. Sometimes when a man is chosen, he cries, and, Susan, sometimes his wife cries even harder!"

A bishop explains the Amish way

What does it mean to be Amish?

> There are many Christian churches in America. Church of God. Assemblies of God, Baptist, Brethren, Christian and Missionary Alliance, Catholic, Lutheran, Presbyterian . . .
>
> But what is the difference between the Amish and these other religious groups? Yes, the Amish dress differently, and their lifestyle is very different from most other religious groups, but is there more?

An Amish bishop and his wife out for a walk.

Some time ago, a group of fifty-two people chartered a bus and came to see the Amish. They had arranged to have an Amish bishop meet them and answer some of their questions.

This was the very first question asked: "We all go to church"—the person asking the question named some of the above churches—"so we all know about Jesus, but what does it mean to be Amish?"

The Amish bishop thought a bit, and then he asked a question of his own.

"How many of you have televisions and computers and cell phones in your homes?"

Every single person on the bus raised their hand.

"How many of you know that sinful things come in through those televisions and cell phones?"

All fifty-two hands went up in the air. Each person nodded to one another, all agreeing that although there's good that comes through those electronic devices, there is also so much sinfulness.

"All right," the Amish bishop replied. "Now how many of you are going to go home and get rid of those items that bring sin into your home?"

Not a hand went up in the air.

Now that is what it means to be Amish. As a church, if the Amish see or experience something that is not good for them spiritually, they will discipline themselves to do without.

The world in general does not know what it is to do without.[1]

This story illustrates one of the main reasons why the Amish shun modern technology. They know that good can come from a computer, or television, but they also know that there is a lot of sin that comes in through those wires or wavelengths. They use a telephone out of

---

1   Adapted from Levi L. Fisher, *Bedenklich Happenings* (Morgantown, PA: Masthof Press, 2013), 28.

necessity, but they also know a telephone might distract people from work and family. In our community, they are not allowed to have a cell phone or any kind of phone within three hundred feet of their dwelling place. The Amish shun modern appliances because they believe that "idle hands are from the devil." They believe that the more free time people have on their hands, the more likely they might get into trouble. They also believe that hard work is good for people and keeps them out of trouble.

A church that gives

A few years ago, a young Amish man from our community was killed in a mill accident. John left behind a wife named Sarah, five children under the age of thirteen, and one on the way. I asked my Amish friend Lena what would happen to the family financially, since the Amish do not carry insurance. Lena answered, "The church will take care of them."

The church, in an Old Order Amish group, is the entire community. Lena assured me, "We are the church! We will all pitch in and help her until her sons are grown and can financially support her. If everybody gives a little, she will have a lot."

A few days after John was killed, I stopped by Lena's and she asked me what the weather was supposed to be like on Saturday. I said it was going to be cool but dry. Lena said, "Good, because at least ten teams of men are going to Sarah's house to plow her fields, winterize her home and barn, and get her winter supply of coal (to heat her home) and wood (for her to cook with). The women are all going to cook and bake to help feed the men who are taking care of Sarah's farm, and will bring food for Sarah to have enough all winter. I'm glad the weather will be nice for them."

This is community.

This is church.

When there is a need, it is taken care of. Not by a few, but by all.

Lord, help us be a better community and a better church.

Let our eyes see the needs. Let our ears hear the cries. Let our hands pitch in to do the dirty work. The Amish like to say, "Many hands make light work." We all need each other.

Many hands make light work. This field is being plowed by friends and neighbors who have come together to help a woman who lost her husband in a sawmill accident.

Datt's home!

TWO

FAMILY

The Amish father (*Datt*)

Clip-clop.

Clip-clop.

"Datt's home!"

"Andy, you go out to the barn and help Dad unharness Betsy."

"I'll get him a hot cup of coffee."

"Mamm, is the bread ready from the oven? Datt loves it when it's nice and warm."

"Let's get his newspaper ready for him."

"Put Datt's slippers and pipe next to his chair and light the oil lamp so he can see when he reads his paper."

I've come to learn that the Amish family is the foundation of the Amish way of life, and the father is the head of his family. He is not only the primary breadwinner but also the spiritual head of the Amish household. Children look up to their fathers as their leader. Sons are often found tagging along after or working beside their fathers from the time they are small boys until after they are grown men.

The hero

One little Amish boy named Harvey, who was five years old at the time, came out from his Datt's shop when he saw my car pull into his drive. His straw hat fell off as he ran to me, and his curly blond hair flopped in the wind and he grinned from ear to ear. His face was covered with dirt and his hands were smeared with black grease.

He stretched out his arms and turned his hands over as he said, "Susie, look, my hands are so dirty. I was helping Datt in the shop." Harvey was so proud of those dirty little hands because they were helping fix a piece of broken machinery in his father's repair shop.

Those hands looked like his father's hands, and Harvey's father is his hero. In our world, children often worship superheroes like Spider-Man or Iron Man, but I've noticed that Amish children often think of their fathers as their heroes: "My Datt can fix anything!" "My Datt is so strong. He can lift big logs!" "Look at the huge buck that my Datt shot!"

"Train up a child in the way he should go: and when he is old, he will not depart from it."—Proverbs 22:6 KJV

PHOTO BY DENISE GUTHERY, USED WITH PERMISSION.

The teacher

Amish fathers teach their sons how to be men. They teach them a man's role in the Amish home. They teach them how to work hard with their hands, whether they are leading a team of horses into the fields to till the soil, putting on a roof, or building furniture. After the age of fourteen, sons often apprentice under their fathers and learn a trade that will carry them through their entire lives by providing an income for their family.

Amish daughters take pride in helping provide a clean and organized home for their fathers. A daughter shows her love for her father by cooking and baking his favorite foods, sewing, or mending his clothes.

The little ones tell their fathers stories, spell words they learned in school, and sing songs. Children are taught to respect and obey their parents, and they want to make them proud by showing them that they can work hard, just as their parents do.

A father trains his sons to be good workers, good neighbors, and good men of God. Amish boys follow in the footsteps of their fathers. Isn't that what we are all supposed to do—follow in the footsteps of our heavenly Father?

The spiritual head of the home

The very first time I had dinner with an Amish family, Eli, the father, said, "Let us pray." I watched as the eight small children, along with their Mamm and Datt, bowed their heads. I, too, bowed mine and waited for the prayer to begin. I soon realized that the Amish pray silently. I kept my head bowed as the seconds turned into minutes. I began to feel uncomfortable. How do you know when to end? I finally peeked one eye open and saw ten pairs of eyes looking at me. I giggled and lifted my head up, and outspoken as I am, I said, "How do you know when to finish?" The children answered and said, "When Datt clears his throat!" There's something wonderful about the father being the head of the house and leading that prayer. It feels so godly. At the end of the meal, Eli also folded his hands and bowed his head and said, "Let us pray." This time, I heard Datt's signal that the prayer was finished!

As we were washing the dishes after the wonderful home-cooked Amish meal, Eli's wife Lizzie explained why they also pray at the end of every meal: "It's so our children don't get up from the table before the meal is completely over. Our dinnertime is family togetherness time. It is a time for us to talk about our day and to relax and enjoy each other as a family. Our children are not allowed to leave until Eli's after-dinner prayer is over."

Family dinners are so very important. They provide an opportunity for family members to come together in a peaceful setting. Families strengthen their ties and build relationships with one another during mealtimes. A sense of belonging is enforced, and the family bond is made stronger over the family dinner table. Children are heard and parents have a chance to be role models during this sacred time.

Love and respect

Levi is an Amish husband and a father to seven children who look up to him with the utmost love and respect.

On his thirty-seventh birthday, Levi went to work as a carpenter like any other ordinary Friday. But as soon as his children came home from school, they began to put their birthday plan for Datt into action. Twelve-year-old Lydia found the recipe for his favorite cake, chocolate ho ho! She began to gather the ingredients while Esther helped fire up the woodstove. Emma, Anna, and Andy went to the barn to milk all

the cows, including the four that Datt usually milked each evening. Harvey pulled Datt's buggy from the barn and began to make it shiny. Little Eli, who was just four years old, found Datt's boots to polish and clean.

The children hurried as fast as they could to get all the chores done. Datt would be home soon! Mamm was making his favorite meal, chicken with mashed potatoes and stuffing. The house smelled so good, and with the cake cooling on the counter, Esther and Lydia began to make the icing while Andy made homemade ice cream.

Little Eli stood by the window waiting to see Datt's *Gallbuggy* (horse and buggy) come up the lane. The children could not help but giggle and shiver with anticipation, because they knew he would be so excited to see the special meal and cake waiting for him. Everyone agreed that they would wait until after dinner to tell Datt that his chores were done. It would be a great surprise!

"He's coming! He's coming!" Eli shouted. They all huddled behind the kitchen door so when Datt walked through it, they could shout, "Surprise!" They heard the basement door open and then close. They heard the clomp of his heavy work boots as he came up the first three stairs. There, he would remove his boots, coat, hat, and tools and put everything away in its proper spot. (Mamm made sure everything was put away in its proper place!) He washed his hands and then climbed the rest of the stairs and opened the kitchen door. All the children and Mamm shouted, "Surprise!"

Datt laughed with glee as the children led him to his seat at the table. They all stuffed themselves with Mamm's delicious meal, and as the younger girls cleared the dishes off the table, the older girls went to get Datt's birthday cake while the boys went outside to get the ice cream, which was keeping cold in the snow. Oh, how he was surprised to see the beautiful cake lit with candles! And he smiled from ear to ear as everyone sang "Happy Birthday."

After he'd had not one but two slices of cake, Datt rubbed his belly and said, "I think this was my favorite day of the year so far! I wish I could just sit right here with my family, but I've got chores to do. Those cows won't milk themselves!"

He started to get up from the table, but all the smaller children grabbed his hands and wrapped their hands around his waist and said, "Datt, you come sit here in your favorite chair." Little Eli ran to get Datt's footstool so he could rest his tired feet.

"But I have chores to do!" he protested.

"No, you don't, Datt. We did them for you!"

Levi had tears in his eyes and his wife Sara was smiling so brightly. The children also fetched the local newspaper for their father to read while he relaxed in his favorite chair.

You might think I made this story up because it's just so sweet, but this is exactly what happened when I was invited to celebrate Levi's birthday with his family. Later we played a game called horse auction and snacked, laughed, and stayed up way later than any Amish family should have been awake! There were no fancy presents given, but the whole family worked together to give Datt a wonderful birthday. This is love and respect in action.

The Amish mother (*Mamm*)

Although Amish men are the leaders of the home, Amish women are equally valued for their role as wife and mother and for the contributions that they make to their community. Amish women are mothers and managers of the household, and they help make the house a home. They maintain the family garden, sometimes help in the fields if needed, and often find jobs to bring in extra income for the family, such as baking, quilting, sewing, or even running a small business from the home. The mother is often the glue that holds the family together.

Two Amish women varnish a dry sink.

The Amish Mamm is usually the first to wake in the morning and last to go to bed at night. When she awakes, she will light the oil lamp and coal stove, put water in the teakettle, and begin preparing breakfast for her family. Some Amish women will go to the barn and help milk the family cows. My friend Lydia says that morning milking is her most enjoyable part of her day because the entire family is in the barn, talking while milking all together and waiting for the sun to rise.

Mamm will make a hardy breakfast for her husband and children while they finish up the morning chores. She will pack lunches for her husband and sons if they work outside the home and for the younger ones who attend school. She will make a list of all she wants to accomplish for the day and immediately get to work on completing those tasks. After all the day's chores are finished, she might sit down and read a book, or do some sewing, or write a letter. There is not much idle time for an Amish Mamm.

Wise advice from an Amish wife

Mary is married to John, who is a contractor. For about a year, John had been working about sixty miles from home on a construction job. He traveled back and forth by Amish taxi (someone who is paid to drive an Amish crew to a job). John's driver listened to talk radio on his trip to and from Pittsburgh, so therefore John also listened to talk radio on his drives. John also reads a lot of newspapers and had recently read several conservative political books. He values wisdom and intelligence, so he likes to read and learn as much as he can. John told my husband and I how riled up he got when he heard these commenters ranting and raving about politics and such. Each day, he would come home and would spew all he heard to Mary and their children.

Mary said, "John, when you are out in the world, you see and hear many things. I need you to leave those things out of this home and keep them in the world. When you are home, it is family time. You need to talk about family things, and the children need you to be present with them, not in the world."

John nodded his head and softly replied, "You are right, Mary. I'm sorry."

Oftentimes we get caught up in the negativity of the world, and we find ourselves in a cloud of gloom and doom. I have learned from my Amish friends to turn off the television, my computer, and my cell phone and to be present in the moment. There are still so many good things in the world. Sometimes we have to steer our minds and hearts back toward those good things.

A few years ago, I was blessed with a fresh homemade apple pie for my birthday from my Amish friend Sarah. Along with the pie, she gave me a rolled-up piece of paper with a little blue ribbon wrapped around it. I thought it might be the recipe for the pie or perhaps a birthday poem, but instead Sarah gave me some good advice. Written on the paper was this:

Wise Advice from an Amish Wife
(*author unknown*)

Whenever you return a borrowed pie pan, make sure it's got a warm pie in it.

Invite lots of folks to supper. You can always add more water to the soup.

There's no such thing as woman's work on a farm. There's just work.

Make home a happy place for the children. Everybody returns to their happy place.

Keep the kerosene lamp away from the milk cow's leg.

It's a whole lot easier to get breakfast from a chicken than a pig.

Always pat the chickens when you take their eggs.

It's easy to clean an empty house, but hard to live in one.

All children spill milk. Learn to smile and wipe it up.

Homemade's always better'n store bought.

A tongue's like a knife. The sharper it is, the deeper it cuts.

A good neighbor always knows when to visit and when to leave.

A city dog wants to run out the door, but a country dog stays on the porch 'cause he's not fenced in.

Always light birthday candles from the middle outward.

Nothin' gets the frustrations out better'n splittin' wood.

The longer the dress hem, the more trusting the husband.

Enjoy doing your children's laundry. Someday they'll be gone.

You'll never catch a runnin' chicken, but if you throw seed around the back door you'll have a skilletful by supper.

Biscuits brown better with a little butter brushed on 'em.
Check your shoelaces before runnin' to help somebody.
Visit old people who can't get out. Someday you'll be one.
The softer you talk, the closer folks'll listen.
The colder the outhouse, the warmer the bed.

The entrepreneur

Although Amish women's primary role is to take care of the home, they often are also very entrepreneurial. From quilters to rug makers, card makers to bakers, they often find ways to bring in extra income. During the coronavirus pandemic, some women even became mask makers!

In the first spring of the pandemic, I saw the need for masks. I downloaded instructions from the Centers for Disease Control website on how to sew a mask and gave them to my Amish friend Barbara, who owns a quilt shop. "Are you up to the task?" I asked. "You may get very busy making masks for people."

"Oh, Susie, yes, this is something we can do for the community. It would be our honor to help."

I called the local newspaper and let them know that local Amish women had agreed to make masks. Little did I know that the story would be picked up nationally. I began receiving phone calls and emails from all over the United States from people wanting to order the masks. After taking hundreds of orders, I made my way to my friend's home and said, "Ladies, you are going to need more than one sewing machine."

Barbara said, "Susie, can you drive me to my sister's home? I will get Mom and Katie and my three nieces to help." We drove to Katie's house and the girls laughed out loud with glee. "Yes, we'll help!"

Making masks on a foot-powered treadle sewing machine. PHOTO BY SUSAN HOUGELMAN, USED WITH PERMISSION.

Word that Amish women were making masks quickly went viral. They enlisted the help of family and friends and sewed from morning until evening. PHOTO BY SUSAN HOUGELMAN, USED WITH PERMISSION.

We hauled their antique treadle sewing machine in my car, along with three of the girls, and drove back to Barbara's house. We unloaded the sewing machine, and I drove back to pick up Barbara's mom and her sewing machine too. All together in Barbara's home, the women put four foot-powered sewing machines in front of the window of their big room for maximum light, and Barbara, her sister Katie, their mother Linda, and Barbara's oldest daughter Lydia began sewing as fast as their hands and feet would allow. The next oldest daughters, Rachael and Lena, cut fabric while Ella cut elastic. Other daughters waited on customers who came in person to buy masks, and some watched the smallest children so the older women could work. They were all laughing with joy.

Barbara's husband had been out of work for over a month, and because businesses were forced to close and we were quarantined here in Pennsylvania, Barbara had not had even one customer in her shop for a very long time. She prayed that God would supply their needs, and boy, did he ever!

These women sewed masks from sunup to sundown. They shipped them out all over the United States to people who heard about their mask-making business. After weeks went by, Linda pulled me aside and said, "Susie, I want to thank you. Not just for the business and income you've provided for both my daughters' families, but for the memories you've helped us create. We will never forget our mask-making adventure!"

The Amish grandparents (*Mommy* and *Doddy*)

Amish grandparents live in a little house beside or even attached to one of their children's homes. This house is smaller than the average Amish home and is called the Doddy Haus. *Doddy*, or *Dawdy*, means "grandfather" in Pennsylvania Dutch. The grandparents have their

The Doddy Haus in spring.

The Doddy Haus preparing for winter.

independence, yet their children and grandchildren are right next door if they need help. There are no nursing homes or retirement villages in our Amish community. The Amish feel that the elder men or women would feel lonely and uncared for if they were sent away.

There is a Doddy Haus that belongs to a grandfather named Henry. Henry's wife passed away years ago. I drive past this little house nearly every day on my tours, and I often see Henry's grandchildren mowing his grass or hanging his laundry out to dry. Recently, Henry's grandsons built him a new porch for his birthday. It was a delight to see ten boys of all different ages and sizes working together to build this special gift for their grandfather. They even built him a new bench for when friends come to visit.

I can imagine the delight Henry felt, not only from having a brand-new porch, but also from knowing that his family cared enough for him to take care of a task that he could no longer accomplish himself. Now when I drive past Henry's Doddy Haus, I often see him sitting on a rocking chair reading the newspaper or visiting with friends.

Don't you think it would be wonderful to grow old living next door to your family? When I take people from other countries on tours, they often tell me that the way the Amish care for older adults is remarkably similar to how they take care of them in their country. Older parents and grandparents are respected and cared for by all members of the family. They are never taken away to a nursing home, not even when they are ill. In the Amish community, everyone takes turns caring for older members of the family who need particular care. The burden does not lie on just one family member. My Amish friends say, "It is a privilege to care for our older folks. They did so much for us when we were young, it is only right that we care for them when they are old."

I could not agree more. The way the Amish treat their older adults has caused me to change the way I think about taking care of the older generation. I am already preparing my children to have enough property to be able to build a "Doddy" house next door!

I had the privilege of knowing a fine Amish man named Daniel. Daniel was an elder in the Amish church, and was also a grandfather to several of my dear Amish friends. Daniel had been exhibiting some strange behaviors, so his family insisted he see a doctor. It was discovered, after several tests, that Daniel had an inoperable brain tumor. His doctors told him that he had just a few weeks to live. The physicians recommended that Daniel be kept in a nursing home to finish out his final days, but that is not the Amish way. Daniel's family brought him home to spend his final days surrounded by his family and friends who love him the most.

When Amish people receive such a diagnosis, they are sent home but will never be alone during the dying process. Every day, hour, minute, someone will be by their side—oftentimes the room is full of friends and family members.

Daniel's grandchildren shared with me daily updates about his condition, who his visitors were, and what transpired: "Susie, today we put a baby in his lap, and he knew to pat the baby." "Today he was able to drink some tea." "He can't talk anymore." Daniel's sisters, brothers, cousins, nephews, and other family members traveled from all over the Midwest to spend those last days with him. When the good Lord takes me, I hope I am surrounded—like Daniel and our Amish friends—by those who love me most.

I once took two of my favorite Amish *Mommies* ("grandmothers" in Pennsylvania Dutch) to visit their brother Sam. Sam left the Amish

Laundry for days. (There are lots of boys in this Amish family!)

Monday is laundry day. In the winter, the laundry is "freeze dried."

more than fifty years ago, when he was just sixteen years old. The sisters had seen him only two or three times in those fifty years. It was beautiful to witness their reunion, filled with laughter and tears. I loved listening to their stories of childhood, growing up Amish, and then the different paths they took into adulthood.

One of the sisters asked her brother, "How many grandchildren do you have now?"

He replied, "Six."

Liz said, "Oh, you've got a lot of catching up to do with me. I've got thirty-six!"

Without hesitation, Sam quickly shot back, "Lizzie, we have TVs!"

I almost spit out my coffee! Oh, what joy God has brought me through my friendships with the Amish!

My Amish friend Eli told me this story about his grandparents: "My grandparents lived at a time when there was not much extra money to spend on anything other than necessities. They lived in Alabama, just fifty miles from the ocean, but never got to see the ocean. In those days you did not travel for pleasure. After living in Alabama for about fifteen years, my grandfather wanted to return home to New Wilmington. My grandmother did not want to move back. She had made a life in Alabama, and several of her children had established their homesteads there. Susan, do you know how my grandfather got my grandmother to move?" Eli asked me.

"I have no idea," I replied.

"He promised that he'd buy her a new washing machine. She had used a scrub board her whole life to wash all the clothes for her husband and thirteen children. The promise of a new wringer washing machine was how my grandfather got her to come home!"

Children

Jesus said, "Let the little children come to me, and do not hinder them, for the kingdom of heaven belongs to such as these."
—Matthew 19:14

The typical Amish family in the New Wilmington community has about six to eight children. Children are a great blessing and a vital part of the Amish family and community. I am always amazed to see how children never seem to be underfoot in the Amish home. They often tag along with their older siblings or parents, helping or just watching, and the adults do not seem to mind. It is so heartwarming to see a little girl with a child-sized broom sweeping the porch with her Mamm, or a little boy with a miniature tool belt wrapped around his waist, hammering a nail into a board alongside his Datt.

My Amish friend Elizabeth says, "Doing things together allows us to be good examples to our children. We teach them to have an excellent work ethic, and we also want to be spiritual role models for them. If they were away in their rooms or spending time watching television, how would they learn our values? We want our children to learn from us, not the world."

We often are so busy and find it difficult to spend time with our children, who are often perched in front of a television, computer, or phone or playing video games. Where are our children learning their values from? Who are their role models? We could learn a lot from the example of the Amish.

One of the families that I visit on my Amish tours has seven children. The five oldest are school-age, and the two youngest are age four and one. I usually stop at this Amish business just a few times per week. When I visit these Amish kids, I bring candy in my car for them, and I love on them with hugs and smiles and silliness. As you can imagine, the children love when they see my car pull up.

One day, their mother said to me, "Susie, we have a problem." Oh no. I was so worried! What had I done wrong? Had I crossed any boundaries? Did they no longer want me to visit? As my mind raced and I thought of the worst, the Amish mama continued, "I can't get Lena"—her four-year-old—"to nap when the kids are at school. She is afraid that you might come while she is sleeping, so she won't go to sleep anymore."

Lena's mother smiled and winked and once again filled my heart with a love for these children and this community that feels like balloon about to burst. They are so precious.

My Amish friend Rebecca is now twelve years old, but she will always be little Becky to me. One time I was visiting her parents' harness shop, and little Becky came running across the parking lot when she saw my car pull in. She was barefoot, but that did not stop her from running as fast as she could. Sweet little red-headed, freckle-faced Becky, with her black Kapp falling off and her dirty little face, was smiling as big of a smile as she could make.

Becky could not speak English at the time, as she was just three years old and most Amish families speak Pennsylvania Dutch at home—many children don't learn English until they go to school. I was still new to the touring business and I did not speak much Pennsylvania

Children are often sent along the back roads with their wagons to do errands for Mamm and Datt.

Amish children often make their own toys and games. This "buggy" was made by a young boy Andy, for his smaller brother and sisters. They rode around the yard with their pony Star for a few weeks until the box fell apart!

Dutch then, but somehow, we communicated with each other. On that day, I was especially excited to see Becky because I had learned a new phrase in the Amish language. Some of the older children had taught me to say "Ich can Dietsch schwetze," which means "I can speak Dutch!"

Becky greeted me with that beautiful smile and said, "Hi, Susie! Vee bisht doo?" (How are you?)

I replied, "Gut, Becky." I was so excited to surprise her with the new phrase that I had learned, so I looked at Becky and continued, "Becky, ich can Dietsch schwetze!"

That little freckled-faced girl didn't miss a beat. She looked at me and replied, "Susie, ich can English schwetze!" (Susie, I can speak English!)

Oh, I belly laughed! I guess we both knew each other's language without having to speak the same words! Love can overcome many barriers.

Respect and obey

From an early age, Amish children are taught to respect and obey their elders. From what I have witnessed in my experiences with the Amish, the older you become, the more respect you are given. Instead of older adults being pushed aside and their old-fashioned beliefs and ways mocked, the older Amish generations are highly honored and respected. I have also noticed that children are not the center of attention in the Amish world. They are taught to put others before themselves. When I pass out candy, they will often say, "May I have one for my brother or sister?" If there is not enough to go around, they will say, "That's okay, little Danny can have it." It is so refreshing and seems to be opposite of how many of our children behave.

When I have dinner with Amish families, it is wonderful to be able to have a conversation with the adults. The children sit and listen quietly. It is rare for an adult conversation to be interrupted by a child, and if it is, the parents will softly ask the child to wait until they are finished talking.

Amish children are usually surrounded by siblings, cousins, aunts, uncles, and grandparents, so they always feel a sense of belonging. In an Amish home, there is no need for playdates or to invite friends over. Amish children do not often get bored, and there is always someone around for them to play with.

One day I took an Amish friend to lunch, and during our conversation she asked, "Susie, did you read a book to the kids called *The Gingerbread Man?*"

I did! Each year around Christmastime, I have a book drive for Amish children. People from all over the United States send boxes of books for me to distribute to Amish schools and families. *The Gingerbread Man* was one of those books.

My friend said, "On Sunday night the grandchildren were visiting and suddenly Jake, their father, got up and started running stiff-legged and stiff-armed, and we looked at him as though he had lost his mind! Then the kids all screamed and started chasing him, and he called out 'Run, run as fast as you can, you cannot catch me, I'm the gingerbread man!' Well, my husband and I started laughing so hard, watching him run that way and seeing all of the children follow behind, that my stomach is still sore!"

She went on to tell me that the children had been playing that game since Christmas and were having so much fun! She said, "Susie, you are creating such wonderful experiences for our children and family. We are so glad that you are our friend!"

PHOTO BY BRIAN SCHMITT, USED WITH PERMISSION.   PHOTO BY TATIANA ILINA/GETTY

It warmed my heart to see something so simple—giving a family a book—bring so much joy! I thanked the Lord for giving me the opportunity to serve him by loving on this incredible family and community. I often tell people, "Bloom where you are planted." I happen to be incredibly fortunate to be able to bloom among an Amish community.

Responsibility

Amish children are also taught a sense of responsibility at an early age. They are given chores beginning around the age of five. They often wake before sunrise and start their day with their chores. Making their bed and tidying up their room is first. Feeding the horses, cats, dogs, chickens, and rabbits and milking the cows all

A family harvests pumpkins together.

takes place before breakfast. Other children will collect eggs and bring them to Mamm, who will cook them up on her woodstove for the first meal of the day.

Chores are not done alone in an Amish family; everybody works together. It is common to see entire families in the fields picking pumpkins or strawberries, gathering hay or corn, or doing yard work.

By the time children reach their teenage years, they typically take over many of the responsibilities or chores of the adults. The girls cook, clean, do laundry, and sew, while the boys tend to the farm, care for the horses, and usually begin working a full-time job, often beside their fathers.

Amish families work together to create a strong bond and sense of accomplishment.

PHOTOS BY BRIAN SCHMITT, USED WITH PERMISSION.

Fun

People often ask me what Amish children do for fun. In the warmer months, the little children have swings and sandboxes and ponies with carts and wagons. And because there are usually many siblings, they always have each other to play with!

In the winter, they love to sled and ice-skate, build snowmen, and play games in the snow like "fox and geese." The children play outside in the fresh air no matter what season of year it is. They are hardy children and enjoy being outdoors more than indoors.

I have spent many evenings in Amish homes singing, playing card games and board games, working on puzzles, and even reading books aloud together. Family time is especially important, and Amish children enjoy spending time together with their siblings, parents, and even grandparents.

The Amish of Lawrence County are not permitted to own cell phones, nor can they have a landline phone within a few hundred yards of their home. Sometimes they need to use a telephone to make an appointment, call a taxi driver, or maybe even contact a doctor or hospital. Located all throughout the Amish community are phone shanties, which are small wooden booths that contain a telephone. An Amish community member can walk to the phone shanty or take a horse and buggy, tie it to a nearby tree, and go inside to make phone calls. Phone shanties are generally used for necessity rather than pleasure.

Nearly every day in April 2020, when the coronavirus pandemic meant we couldn't visit friends as we usually would, I received a phone call from eight-year-old Amanda and her five-year-old sister Esther, who walked to the nearby phone shanty to call me. They had found my number on a business card given to their parents and memorized it.

"Hello, Susie," they would say, and I would reply with a giggle, "Who is this?" (I knew who was calling but I loved to hear them say it.)

"It's Amanda." In the background, another giggling voice said, "And me too, Susie, it's Esther!"

Every time I would say, "Amanda and Esther who?"

They would giggle some more and say, "Amanda and Esther Byler!"

"Oh, I'm not sure I know anyone with those names."

And every single time they would say, "Susie, yes, you do! We are at the harness shop!"

"Oh, *that* Amanda and Esther, the two silly girls at the harness shop!" And they would giggle some more.

Every day they would tell me what events had happened: "Becky fell and hurt her arm. Johnny is training the new pony, but he's still bucking. We're having pizza tonight for Datt's birthday. Mamm's making ice cream. Strawberry's my favorite!"—pronounced "favor-right"—"Susie what's your favor-right?" "Chocolate? Rebecca likes chocolate too."

I would listen and laugh, and at the end of every call I would say, "Amanda and Esther, I love you and I miss you."

Sometimes they would say, "I love you and miss you too, Susie," and sometimes they would just say, "Okay." Oh, my heart!

A phone booth in use. PHOTO BY SUSAN HOUGELMAN, USED WITH PERMISSION.

THREE

COMMUNITY

"Love the Lord your God with all your heart and with all your soul and with all your mind and with all your strength." The second is this: "Love your neighbor as yourself." There is no commandment greater than these.
—Mark 12:30-31

THE AMISH COMMUNITY shows the world how to "love your neighbor as yourself." They share one another's burdens. If one has a need, the entire community will pull together to help! From babysitting each other's children to helping with financial needs, to caring for each other when one is ill, to helping each other build their houses, this group of people comes together. The Amish put community above the individual and live out the biblical command in John 13:34 to "love one another as [Christ has] loved you."

Barn raisings

Few burdens are heavy if everybody lifts.
—Amish proverb

Oh, how I love to watch an Amish barn raising! The men in the community will give up one and sometimes two day's wages to close their shops down and stop what they are working on at home to help their friend in need. If they have a family member in another state who needs help, they will rent one or two buses to take fifty to one hundred men to help plan, organize, and manually build the barn! Women will take time away from their daily household chores to help cook a feast for the hardworking men.

A local Amish family was having a barn raising, and I was invited to watch. I pulled my car into the Amish lane at six-thirty in the morning, but I was not the first to arrive. There were over thirty brown-topped buggies lined up in the side yard, and just as many horses grazing in the pasture. There were horse and buggies clip-clopping down the lane, one after another, some of them parking at a nearby neighbor's. It seemed like every man had a tool in his hand and every woman a basket of food or a pie. Nobody came empty-handed.

I joined the women as they unloaded pans of roasted chicken, mashed potatoes, and stuffing into the Amish home. There the women would spend all morning and afternoon preparing and cooking lunch and then dinner for all those who came to help with the barn raising. I said to my friend Anna, who had invited me to the barn raising, "I think there will be enough food here to feed an army!"

Anna laughed and said, "Susan, there will be an army here to feed. An army of hungry barn builders! These men know they will be fed a delicious meal with several desserts at the end of their workday. It gives them incentive to work hard, knowing they will be well fed."

An Amish barn raising.

The children of the men and women gathered together in the yard, the older ones keeping an eye on the young ones, playing games and singing and laughing, excited for the community project to begin. At a barn raising, even the children will help by completing small tasks and errands for the fathers and mothers who have come to help. There is no fighting or crying among the children and no need for adult supervision.

I watched as the men organized together into small groups, led by two "engineers" who laid out the plans for the barn and who made sure the materials were gathered and available for use. Soon the men broke up and began to work on building the barn. The sound of hammers and saws, along with the shouts of men as they communicated with one another, reverberated throughout the farm. It was astounding to watch and listen to this group of people work. Younger men climbed on top of the barn frame while older men passed up boards to them. Some were whistling and all seemed to be smiling as they worked.

The community comes together to build a barn.

Amish women watch the barn raising.

Inside the Amish farmhouse, the women talked in English (so as not to be rude to their English guest) and giggled and gossiped as they shared local news of the community with one another. The smell of the roasting chicken filled the air as I, along with several other women, peeled potatoes, chopped vegetables, and prepared the heaping bowls of food that would soon be served. One of the women said to me, "Susan, are you sure you owned a restaurant? You seem to be having a hard time peeling those potatoes."

They all laughed as I told them it was my husband's job at our restaurant to peel the potatoes; my job was to smile and say hello to people! "Oh!" they replied. "So you are a spoiled wife!"

Then they all laughed again, and I stuck my tongue out at them, which made them laugh even harder. My Amish friends have such good senses of humor and like to make their work lighter by laughing and having fun.

The younger Amish women in the group set up plastic tables with wooden benches on each side. They put white plastic coverings on each table and at each setting a paper plate, eating utensils, and a Styrofoam cup.

Before I knew it, it was noontime. Ruth, the woman of the house, rang the dinner bell, and everything came to a complete stop. The women carried steaming platters of the roasted chicken and bowls of mashed potatoes, stuffing, gravy, corn, and several other Amish side dishes. There were at least forty pies and different desserts. There was so much food that it made me laugh. We served a lot of people in our restaurant, but never 150 people at one time. It was equally as amazing to me to watch the women cook and serve that many hungry people as it was to watch the men build the barn.

As I helped serve, I listened as the men shared stories of hunting, fishing, livestock auctions, and other barn raisings. It seemed as if they were filling their souls as well as their bellies. After the meal was over, the women gathered up the dirty bowls and platters. They and the children took turns sitting and eating while others washed and dried the dishes and cleaned the tables. New tablecloths were put on and platters of cookies and cakes, along with pitchers of juice and bottles of soda, were placed on the tables for an afternoon break.

As the afternoon turned into evening, a brand-new barn stood in the farmer's field, and one by one the men collected their tools as they finish the last tasks. The women gathered up their children along with the dishes they had brought, and it was time to say goodbye. Horses were rounded up and soon the buggies left for home. My back was tired and my hands a bit sore as my eyes welled with tears. My heart was full from seeing and experiencing firsthand the love the Amish community has for one another. As I said goodbye to Anna and thanked her for inviting me to the barn raising, she handed me a basket filled with food for my husband and said, "Susan, it is our honor to help one another. Someday we know it will be our turn to need help. Thank you for your help."

❦

Husking bees

A husking bee is an old Amish tradition that dates back to the 1800s. The husking bee is usually hosted by a family that needs to harvest a lot of corn but doesn't have enough family members to help. So they invite their friends and neighbors over with the promise of a satisfying meal and a fun time after the work is done.

My Amish friends recently had a husking bee and invited about one hundred people, who brought six teams of horses with wagons. With everyone working, it took just three and a half hours to walk up and down the rows in six acres of corn and pick all the corn. After the work was over, the host family provided homemade meatloaf, mashed

potatoes and gravy, applesauce, two different casseroles and, oh, the desserts . . . apple pie, cherry pie, peanut butter pie, and cookies galore!

After everybody is well fed, the fun begins. The older Amish folk, and younger ones, all cheer and clap while the single young Amish men and women sing and square dance. It is truly a harvest party and a remarkable sight! My friends' party lasted until midnight. Everyone involved was tired the next morning, but it was a good kind of tired to be.

Many hands make light work! Neighbors helping neighbors. Family and friends gathering to help one another. And they make a party out of it. Don't you wish our world was more like this? That is the way it should be!

A little bit of love
can be like sunshine after rain.
And cause someone to realize

that life is not in vain.
We never know how very much
a bit of love can do.
And as we cheer another's heart
our own gets lighter, too.
—*Anonymous*

Our Amish friends surround one another with love.

There was an eighteen-year-old Amish boy in Pittsburgh who fell off a roof and was paralyzed, and during the many weeks he was in the hospital, his family would not leave his side. Well, they would not leave the waiting room, except to sleep and eat. You see, only one family

Corn shocks are a sure sign of fall in Amish country.

member (the boy's father) was allowed in to see Danny because of COVID-19. But the entire family still surrounded the hospital, making sure he was never alone. His girlfriend, who was also eighteen, called him every single day, even though he could not talk because of a tracheal tube. She would talk to him for an hour, encouraging him and telling him that she loved him and needed him to get better.

Danny was in the hospital and rehab for more than a month, and his medical bills were more than his family could afford. Danny's friends decided that they were going to help pay them. Three young men put together a bow shoot. The local auction barn donated the facility. The boys hung up flyers all throughout the Amish community. The event was the talk of the neighborhood that week. I saw many teenage boys and a few men practicing with their bows and arrows.

The day of the bow shoot arrived, and I decided to take a lawn chair and go and watch the activities. I was one of only three women in attendance.

Danny's friends brought in hundreds of bales of hay and pinned targets all over the hay bales. Behind each target was a prize. The prizes were knives, hunting gear, flashlights, and many little items that Amish men would like to have. There were some big prizes, too, like a new crossbow. I think just about every man and boy in the Amish community was at the auction barn that evening to support Danny and his family in need. Each shot was twenty dollars, and I saw many men buy five to ten shots. I was in awe of their generosity and the love they have for each other.

You are never alone in the Amish community. They share each other's sorrows. They help each other in times of need. They are never too busy or too tired to help or to love. We could learn so much from our Amish friends.

Auctions

Every year on the first Saturday in June, our Amish community has a benefit auction. This is a favorite day of the year for many Amish and English community members. Each Amish family donates their time (by working at the auction) or their talent (building, baking, sewing, or growing something to donate) or their treasure (money and auction items to donate) to raise money for medical bills in the community. There is a board of directors, chosen every four years, that oversees the auction, and a different church district works the auction each year.

Nearly every Amish community member, children included, attends the auction, as well as thousands of Amish and English visitors. All the money raised will go toward the medical bills of a community member. It is fun to see the women and young girls serving pizza and other homemade goodies. The men and boys are usually gathered around the horse auction barn or wherever there are tools and other equipment.

The women gather in the quilt auctioning barn. The Amish women from each church district will spend time together hand-stitching a

Auctions provide a place to socialize. PHOTO BY DENISE GUTHRIE, USED WITH PERMISSION.

Folks gathered at the auction site. PHOTO BY DENISE GUTHRIE, USED WITH PERMISSION.

Handsewn quilts are displayed behind the auctioneer, and everyone is curious to see which quilts raise the most money. PHOTO BY DENISE GUTHRIE, USED WITH PERMISSION.

Young boys among the buggies parked outside the auction. PHOTO BY JAN SUMNER, USED WITH PERMISSION.

quilt for the auction. The most beautiful quilts get hung up above the auctioneer. The women are anxious to see which quilts were chosen to be hung, and of course it is the talk of the town to see whose quilt fetches the highest price!

It is also fun to see the hundreds of buggies lined up in the fields next to the auction site. People will often ask me, "How do they know which buggy is theirs, when they all look the same?"

I asked my Amish friends, and they said, "Every buggy has an identifying mark, whether it's a dent from a horse kick or a scratch on a reflector. It is easy for us to know which buggies are ours. Sometimes we will stick a marker like a soda can under our buggies just to be sure."

I cannot help but wonder myself whether anyone has accidentally taken the wrong buggy home from the auction, and whether they would know it if they did. I know that they often sew their initials underneath their hats and inside their cloaks to identify them, so perhaps they do something similar with the buggies.

♥

Boxes of love

Have you ever heard of an ABC box?

My Amish friend Lena, who was just twenty-two years old, arrived home from the hospital. It was discovered, after a check for pneumonia, that Lena had a hole in her heart. She had surgery to fix the hole, was hospitalized for a week, and was then sent home to rest for six weeks. It is exceedingly difficult for an Amish person to rest, but doctor's orders!

Lena's church district, which is made up of her family, friends, and neighbors, decided to help Lena make her six weeks more bearable. Each family was given a letter from *A* to *Z*, and they had to fill a box with items that begin with the letter they were given. For example, the family with the letter *C* put candy, crayons, cotton balls, and crackers in the box for their friend.

The boxes were collected at one location and delivered to Lena's porch. Lena's face was overflowing with excitement as the boxes were set on her porch right in front of her bedroom window. Imagine the love she felt knowing that she was thought of and cared for during this time of bedrest.

Lena was allowed to open one box each day, starting with the letter *A*. She would have twenty-six days (about three and a half weeks) of excitement, helping her have something to look forward to during this time of healing.

I am so happy to report that Lena did have her baby and both mama and child are healthy and happy!

Another way the Amish "love thy neighbor" is to give hurting people or families in need a shower box, which they sometimes call a sunshine box. A cardboard box is placed inside an Amish store with the person or family's name written on it, as well as a note that says something like this: "Eli Byler fell off a roof and cannot work for six weeks. Let us shower their family with kindness and help with necessities."

A sunshine box might say, "Mary Byler is a widow and could use some sunshine to brighten her days. Let us fill this box and bring some sunshine to Mary."

A grocery shower box. PHOTO BY SUSAN HOUGELMAN, USED WITH PERMISSION.

Friends, I have witnessed those boxes be filled up in one day and replaced with another empty box to be filled. The Amish are such a generous, kind, and loving group of people. Truly, it is so simple. Why have we made life so complicated?

♥

Acts of kindness

Over lunch one day, I was sharing with my young Amish friend Esther some stories about a recent vacation, and I asked if she did anything fun while I was away.

She said, "Yes! I did two fun things. The first fun thing I did was attend a birthday party for a lady whose husband and son left her to join the English. She is incredibly sad and lonely, so every family in our church district decided to surprise her with a birthday party. Each family used four toilet paper tubes and filled them with little surprises. In ours, we put batteries and candy, buttons and money, hairpins, a small bottle of lotion, and a pair of socks. We wrapped up each tube like a tootsie roll, but we used pretty paper and ribbon to tie each end. Each family also brought something good to eat to the party. Boy, was Nancy shocked when she saw everybody was there for her, and she could barely talk when she was given one hundred tootsie rolls filled with surprises!"

Oh, dear reader, my heart just flutters at the beauty of how the Amish love one another and make sure nobody is ever left out.

The other fun thing my young Amish friend did that week? Her whole family cleaned up all the overgrown brush around their pasture fence. She said it was such a beautiful day and it was so much fun because the whole family was together outdoors enjoying the sunshine! Could you imagine another thirteen-year-old sharing those two events as the fun she had over the weekend?

My friend Andy was extremely sick. He visited several doctors, but they were unable to diagnose his condition. He began to feel so ill that he could not get out of bed. Andy owned an eighty-acre farm where he raised beef cattle and grew corn. When it came time to harvest the corn, Andy was unable to perform the task.

One day, I went to visit Andy and bring him some homemade soup. I pulled into his long lane and I saw at least six teams of horses with many men and children out in Andy's field. I saw women scattered all over his yard and on his porch, washing windows, sweeping, painting, and attending to other jobs.

Teamwork makes the dream work. PHOTO BY BRIAN SCHMITT, USED WITH PERMISSION.

Andy's mom came out to greet me. "Ada, what is going on?" I asked.

"Oh, Susie," she replied with tears in her eyes, "these are all Andy's brothers and sisters and their families. They heard Andy was sick, so they came from three different states to help."

"Did you know they were coming?" I replied.

"No, we didn't. It was a surprise." The power of love in action is a beautiful sight to see.

There was a little nine-year-old girl in a neighboring Amish community who was burned when her parents' stove exploded. After coming home from the hospital, she was greeted with many brightly colored boxes and bags of sweets, books, and toys from Amish families from several different communities.

Perhaps an even greater gift to the little girl and her family was what happened the night she came home and each night for several months after that. Each evening, one woman from our Amish community would visit the little girl and rub coconut oil and other healing balms on her body. Each church district took turns sending a representative, so the gift of compassion was shared by the entire community.

Dear reader, when writing these stories to share with you, I often have tears in my eyes as I remember these amazing acts of kindness and love shown by the Amish community toward one another. This story brought the most tears. Not only was the little girl shown love, care, and compassion, but it relieved a great burden from her family. Someone was there every night to sit and keep their mind off the horrific accident. Oh, we have much to learn from our Amish friends about how to love our neighbors.

Financial help

When an Amish family is having a challenging time making ends meet, the community will band together and help. The Amish not only tithe their money (one day's wages go to their church each month, and all that money helps pay for needs in the community, such as medical bills, assisting widows, and so on) but also donate by fundraising, passing the hat (when a particular need arises, a literal hat is passed around to each member of the church and members will put in what they can afford), and other clever ways of supporting one another.

The money tree

My Amish friend Sylvia told me this story of how she helped raise money for a family to pay for treatment for their son who had a seizure disorder. Benny is a young man with mental and physical disabilities who suffers from daily seizures. Benny loves money, so on holidays or special occasions, Benny's family always gives him a card with money tucked inside as his gift. Sylvia said it's so much fun to see his face light up and watch him scream with excitement when he receives this gift—even if it's just one dollar—that friends and family members like to give him money just to watch his reaction! But Benny's family did not have the money needed to travel to Wisconsin to receive a new treatment that may have helped their son with his seizures.

My friend Sylvia got an idea. She went outside and collected a tree limb with lots of little branches attached, then "planted" this tree limb in a red pot. She sent a letter to each family in her church district and asked if they would help donate to Benny's family. She bought a pack of little red envelopes, and inside each envelope, she put money that was donated. That tree was covered with little red envelopes! This "money tree" was given to Benny as a present, but really the money was for his family to help with their financial burden.

Sylvia said that Benny couldn't even sit down after opening his gift. He kept jumping up and down and clapping his hands together while screaming with joy and excitement. His parents' smiles seemed never-ending. The entire family, filled with gratitude and thanksgiving, cried tears of joy. Thanks to the help of their loving neighbors, Benny and his family were able to travel to Wisconsin and he was able to see the specialists he needed.

What special ways can you find to help your neighbors or friends in need? It is fun to think outside the box, and it makes the giver's heart as happy as the receiver's to spread such kindness and love.

Peddling pizzas

One afternoon while I was touring the Amish countryside, I saw a young Amish woman and man delivering pizzas and subs to every Amish home that I visited. They were riding in a van with a sign that said, "Please buy a pizza or sub to help Wally Byler, who has cancer." The back of the van was filled with pizzas and subs. Every single Amish family I visited that Saturday bought at least four pizzas and several subs.

I asked my Amish friend Lydia what the van was doing. She said, "Susan, that's one of the ways that we fundraise for a family in need. Not only does it raise money, but we, especially us women, love the opportunity to buy pizza and subs because that means we don't have to cook dinner that night!"

About every Amish family in New Wilmington had the same meal that evening, and Wally Byler's family was able to feel relieved that their loved one would be cared for.

From barn raisings and frolics to corn huskings and plowings, if an Amish person or family needs help, they are surrounded by church members and neighbors to help. The Amish put community above the individual and believe that God ordained them to love and help one another. Don't you think our world would be a much better place if we all helped one another as the Amish do?

PHOTO BY BRIAN SCHMITT, USED WITH PERMISSION.

FOUR

SCHOOL TIME

THERE ARE two distinct types of lessons to teach: how to make a living and how to live. The Amish value how they live over how they make a living.

Amish children attend school in one-room schoolhouses. Every church district (made up of about twenty-five families) has its own schoolhouse. Children go to school from first grade (age six) to eighth grade (age fourteen). Instead of backpacks, the Amish children carry insulated lunch boxes to school. Books, pencils, tablets, and crayons are all kept at school. Most Amish children walk to school, soaking in that fresh air and getting their exercise before school starts. If they live far away, the public school district provides transportation.

The teacher in an Amish schoolhouse is usually an unmarried young woman who has no formal training beyond her own eighth-grade education. Once women are married, they often do not want to work outside of the home—an Amish wife has enough work to do inside her own home!

Inside an Amish schoolhouse

I have a young Amish friend who is a schoolteacher. Lavina is eighteen years old. She graciously allowed me to come inside her little white schoolhouse with the cheerful, bright blue door as she finished her day's schoolwork. I felt as though I was walking into the old schoolhouse where Miss Beadle taught Laura and Mary Ingalls in *The Little House on the Prairie*. Old-fashioned desks, all facing the larger teacher's desk, sat in neat rows inside the cozy one-room schoolhouse. Lavina

A one-room Amish schoolhouse.

Looking into an Amish schoolhouse. PHOTO BY JAN SUMNER, USED WITH PERMISSION.

explained that younger children sit up front so they can receive the most help, and older children sit in the back.

There was an old chalkboard, and hung above it were two rows of alphabet letters. Lavina said that the younger children learn their English ABCs, and the older children learn their German ABCs. When Amish children come to school for the first time, they only know how to speak Pennsylvania Dutch, which is the language spoken in all Amish homes. Once they begin school, the first order of business is to learn to speak English.

Lavina said, "We allow the children to speak Dutch in the first year of school, but by the second grade, and up until eighth grade, they are only allowed to speak English in school." She continued, "Before school begins, the children can play outside in the yard. I hear them talking and screaming in Pennsylvania Dutch, but as soon as the eight o'clock bell rings, they switch to English. It is the same when the three o'clock bell rings when school is over. They will instantly stop talking in English and switch back to Pennsylvania Dutch."

Lavina also told me that the children learn very quickly. She said, "Susie, by Christmas most Amish children are learning to read and write in English. By the end of the school year, they can completely read and write in English."

I asked Lavina if they also learn to read and write in Pennsylvania Dutch. She shook her head and smiled. "Pennsylvania Dutch is just a spoken language. We don't read or write in Pennsylvania Dutch."

"Lavina," I asked, "how do parents read books to their children when they are young, before they attend school?"

She answered, "Parents will interpret the books themselves into our language for the children."

Cloaks and coats await the recess break. PHOTOS BY JAN SUMNER, USED WITH PERMISSION.

ABOVE PHOTOS BY JAN SUMNER, USED WITH PERMISSION.

A schoolhouse in the fall. PHOTO BY DENISE GUTHERY, USED WITH PERMISSION.

My eyes roamed around the room. Sunlight streamed in through the windows as I tried to take in the simplicity and beauty of the one-room schoolhouse. There was a handmade sign with perfect handwriting that hung above Lavina's desk. It said:

Do you want to feel Joy?
JOY
Jesus First
Others Second
You Last
That's the way to have true joy in life.

I thought to myself, Those are wise words to teach children, and wouldn't the world be a much better place if we adults lived by those words, too?

There were sweet and cheery motivational posters placed about the room, and neatly colored children's artwork hung on all four walls. Lavina explained, "Art is on Fridays. The children enjoy coloring pictures or making a craft to take home."

The schoolteachers use a curriculum published by a Mennonite publishing company in Ohio. I looked through the children's workbooks and I could not help but smile. Most pages were of farms, barns, and animals. I suppose Amish children could not relate to many of the modern storybooks that our English children read today.

The young children learn to read from the same books that I learned to read from in the early 1970s. They are called basal readers, and the main characters in the books are named Dick and Jane. They have a sister named Sally and a dog named Spot. Looking through those readers brought back such memories! These books were in almost every American classroom in the 1960s and '70s and are still used today in Amish classrooms.

Walking to school.

Some of the older children's books are textbooks published from the 1930s through the 1950s. The children are taught basic math skills and history from these books. All the books on their bookshelves were also very old.

Lavina will light the coal stove, which heats the schoolhouse, first thing in the morning. After all the children arrive, she will take attendance. The children will then start the day by reciting the Lord's Prayer in German and singing praises to God. (What a wonderful way to start the day!) The first graders will begin to learn English, and then they will learn to read and write in English. The older students will learn math, spelling, reading, writing, and history, and the older ones will learn High German. The older children often help instruct the younger children.

Amish children learn much more than the basics in school. They also learn the golden rule from Matthew 7:12 ("Do unto others that you would have them do unto you"), discipline, cooperation, respect, and responsibility.

Amish children usually have recess about three times a day—they need to have a place to let that energy go. The children will play baseball and tag, "Johnny come over," and other fun ball games. In the winter, schoolchildren are allowed to sled during recess. When they come in from the cold, they warm up by the coal stove, and sometimes the teacher will offer them a snack and hot cocoa. They will have no homework when school is finished. Instead, there will be chores to do at home.

School games

One weekend, I visited with an Amish schoolteacher friend named Lydia, who told me of a fun activity that was happening in her classroom. One of her student's parents brought in ten different colored balloons, each with a note inside. Lydia told the students that they were to do their very best in school each day. If the teacher agreed that the children had worked hard, she would choose one child to pop a balloon any time after lunch.

Lydia then grinned and said, "Susan, those children were so well behaved, and they got their work completed without a complaint. They could not wait until that balloon was popped! At about two, I took the first balloon, the orange one, and I chose the youngest child in the classroom to come and pop the balloon. You should have seen the look on his face as he came to the front of the classroom. I do not think I have ever seen a child smile so brightly! I gave Harvey a pin, and with one flick of his wrist he popped the orange balloon. The children

School children playing softball. PHOTO BY BRIAN SCHMITT, USED WITH PERMISSION.

laughed at the loud noise it made. The note that the balloon was holding went flying, and Harvey ran after it. He brought it to the front and handed it to me. The note said, 'The three students who did the poorest on their spelling tests today must sweep the classroom for the teacher!' The children exploded in laughter. Little Harvey groaned, knowing that he missed several words on his test that morning, and indeed he was one of my sweepers!"

I could not help but laugh thinking of the excitement those children must have felt, and I could not wait for Lydia to continue.

"The next day was very much the same. The children were very well behaved, and, Susan, the funniest thing happened. Every single student got a 100 percent on their spelling test! Two o'clock came, and this time I chose Rachael, a sweet fifth-grade girl, to pop a green balloon. She used her own pin. I saw some children holding their ears waiting for that pop, and all the children were laughing and bursting with excitement. Rachael pushed the pin into the balloon, and once again the little note inside went flying. I let Rachael retrieve the note and read it aloud to the class. The note said, 'Each student must come to the front of the classroom.' I asked Rachael to pause as all the students hurriedly ran to the front of the room. After the children were gathered up front surrounding Rachael, I saw her eyes sparkle as she finished reading the note. She started giggling so hard she almost could not continue. 'The last one back to their seat has to stand on their chair and say, "Excuse me, but I'm a slow poke!"'

"The children all laughed and ran back to their seats as fast as they could, and it was little Harvey, one of the students who had to sweep the floor on Wednesday, who was the last one back to his seat. Oh, what fun the children were having with this game!"

"What about the next day?" I asked with anticipation. I think I may have been as eager as the children to see what was in the third balloon.

"The next day, a Friday, was just like the previous two. The children were happy and very well behaved. I told the students whoever could answer a math problem first could be the one to pop the purple balloon. It was the oldest boy in the class, an eighth grader named Andy. I gave Andy my pin, and after he popped it he was swift enough to catch the note that was released. The children thought that was funny, too.

"Andy read the note, which said, 'Whoever did something kind for another student today, raise their hand.' The children sat at their desks, and at first nobody raised their hand. Finally, one of my little girls raised her hand and said, 'Ada helped me find my cloak at recess time.' We all looked at Ada, whose cheeks were starting to become bright pink with the attention given to her.

"I asked Ada if she did help Anna find her cloak, and quietly Ada replied, 'Yes.'

"'Well, that was truly kind of you. Thank you, Ada,' I told her. 'Anybody else do something kind today?' Nobody raised their hand or responded, so I asked Andy to continue reading the note.

"'If you did something kind today for another student, you may choose something in the goodie bag that I have given your teacher,' he read.

"Along with the balloons, this parent did indeed deliver a bag filled with candy. Ada came to the front of the room smiling ear to ear and picked a pack of gum from the goodie bag."

"Oh, Lydia," I laughed, "I bet the children can't wait for Monday to come to see what surprise the balloon will carry!"

Lydia responded, "Susan, what is incredible is this little game has really helped the children to do their best on tests, and to be well behaved and kind to each other!"

What a clever idea. It's so simple, and so inexpensive. It is ten days' worth of fun for the schoolchildren, and it really did help them do their best at school.

We make things so complicated, when sometimes it is the simple things that bring so much joy.

Holiday celebrations

Amish schoolchildren celebrate holidays in school. Sometimes these holiday celebrations are held after the holiday so the teacher can buy candy for her students at a discounted price.

For Valentine's Day, the children will have a special party at school. They exchange names with another student and make a special handmade card at home for that student. (Mamm usually helps the younger ones.) Girls will make valentines for girls and boys will make valentines for boys. Girls' valentines will have paper hearts and flowers attached, while boys will often draw a deer or horse on their valentines. They will write their own verses on the valentines, such as, "Roses are red, violets are pink, you smell like a skunk, you sure do stink!" (That's actually the verse on the back of a valentine that my little Amish friend Ada showed me!) The children will also make paper hearts for their teacher. The teacher buys candy and makes valentines for each of the

A special valentine made by an Amish schoolgirl. PHOTO BY SUSAN HOUGELMAN, USED WITH PERMISSION.

students. Often, the Amish parents will bring in special goodies for the children to eat.

For Easter, the children sing sweet songs of spring and memorize poems about Easter. They make Easter baskets out of plastic and yarn, which the teacher fills with candy. Each child will bring a dozen hard-boiled eggs from home—some will be dyed, and others will just be brown eggs, most likely freshly hatched from their own chickens! The teacher will hide the eggs in the schoolyard, and at recess the children will run to find them. Although Amish children are not taught to be competitive, they know exactly who found the most eggs and who found the least!

Instead of having several vacation days from school during the holidays, Amish children usually only get the actual holiday itself off from school. Instead, they take a fall break the first week of October. They call that harvest week. During harvest week, many children will help their parents or extended family members pick corn and help prepare their farms for winter.

An Amish children's Christmas program

The children spend several weeks before Christmas memorizing their lines for the much-anticipated children's Christmas program. Mamm and Datt and the older *Kinner* (children) help. Each night after dinner, the children practice saying the words exactly right and getting rid of the shyness or giggles that might come with standing in front of a crowd. The little ones have just a few lines to say, and the older children memorize long verses and stories. The teacher assigns students a song or poem according to each child's ability. Some of these poems and stories are in German and some are in English. The children also learn Christmas songs, and some are in German and some in English.

On Christmas Eve, the little schoolhouse is filled with parents, grandparents, and siblings who have all come to see the children sing and recite their special poems. The coal stove is lit, the schoolhouse is decorated with all the pretty pictures the children have made, and the teacher is as nervous as the children, hoping they all do well!

And so the Christmas program begins:

Harvey (age six):
> I'm the first one in the program.
> It's the most important part.
> For you wouldn't have a program
> if you didn't have a start.

Andy (age seven):
> Well! I am glad to see you here!
> I have a piece to say,
> but all I've done is practice it
> to empty seats each day.
> So here it is, now that you're here:

We welcome you today.
We want you all to feel at home.
Now did I do okay?

Rachael (age seven):
Christmas Thanks
We always remember, I hope,
to say a "thank you much"
for all our Christmas presents,
books, dolls, skates, and such.
And so I'm thinking now
of the great thanks we owe
for that wondrous gift of God
the first Christmas long ago.

Eli (age seven):
My Mamm says that every time
I'm cross or rude or play
an extra game, it makes her hair
turn a little bit more gray.

Parents gathered for an Amish children's school Christmas program.

But when my Mamm was a little girl
she must have been a fright,
for dear old Grandmother's hair
is absolutely white!

This one, from Sylvia (age eight), starts my tears flowing:
Christmas Prayer
Dear Father up in heaven,
upon this Christmas night,
I fear there are some children
whose Christmas is not bright.
For there are some who sorrow
and there are some who sigh.
Now such as these, dear Father,
the Christmas may pass by.
If there are any children
in barren rooms or drear,
whose little empty stockings
hold not a sign of cheer,
O Father, send the Christ child
into these hearts so sad,
and may his living presence
make their Christmas season glad.

David (age eight):
I made my mother a present
to give to her on Christmas Day.
I took a piece of plywood
and turned it up this way.
I pasted on a picture
nailed on a writing pad,
drilled a hole to hang it up
and tied on a pencil I had.

I wrapped it up real pretty.
It only cost me fifteen cents.
But I can't tell you what it is,
because Mother is in the audience.

Lydia (age eight), holding a cutout sign that says JOY:
I've heard it said that joy's a word
that, when taken letter by letter,
can make us understand just how
such a small word can make things better.
The *J*, of course, is for Jesus,
the *O*, why that means others,
the *Y* means you come last yourself,
after all your sisters and brothers.
So when you're putting Jesus first
in everything you do
then it really is no wonder
that others see joy in you!

The program goes on, but I will share just one more because it is so touching!
Andy (age ten):
How can we celebrate Christmas
in a world so troubled and torn,
where men who were made in his image
are forgetting that Jesus was born?
Born to bring peace where there's conflict,
born to bring love where there's hate,
born to die for the sinner
and open the heavenly gates.
To all who will kneel before him,
who was born in a humble stall,
to all who will stop and listen

and come when they hear him call,
oh, how can we celebrate Christmas
today on this war-torn earth?
By living for him and sharing with others
the good news of his birth!

The Amish children then sing their sweet Christmas carols and songs, and then the program is over. Everyone feels relieved, and then the fun can begin! Parents have brought goodies for all to share, and the teacher has planned games for the children to play all afternoon. There are candies and sweets for everyone. Each child has chosen a name of another child, and gifts are exchanged. Sometimes children receive as much as they will on Christmas Day: new fabric for dresses, a little cedar chest with a picture of a wolf or buck, a new knife, a little trash can with pretty flowers and the child's name stenciled on it. The teacher also gifts each child with a special present, and in return the parents of the children bring gifts for the teacher, including financial blessings for her this Christmas.

It warms my heart to witness the simplicity, beauty, and love poured into an Amish school Christmas program.

The end-of-school picnic

For the last day of school, parents and siblings of each student come to the schoolhouse for a picnic. The teacher makes an outdoor fire, and the parents help grill hamburgers. Some mothers bring salads, casseroles, and desserts for everyone to enjoy. Homemade ice cream is always a favorite. The children play outdoor games like sack races and balloon stomps, and small prizes are handed out for the winners. For the children who had perfect attendance, the teacher awards them with a beautiful,

hand-decorated plate with the student's name and year on it. These plates will be displayed on each child's dresser until the children leave home. The teacher also passes out gifts to the children for the last day of school, and the children's parents often bless the teacher with monetary gifts.

New school

One of the little one-room schoolhouses in New Wilmington sat on the corner of a rather busy intersection. The parents of the schoolchildren felt that the school was too close to the main roadway, and with the trouble happening in our world today, they felt it would be safer if the schoolhouse was moved to another location.

One of the parents in our community donated a piece of land, but instead of moving the old schoolhouse, the parents decided to build a new one. All the fathers of the schoolchildren got together over a couple of Saturdays (in between harvesting their corn and other fields) and pitched in to build the structure. Then the mothers of the schoolchildren painted it, made new curtains, and varnished the floors. They finished it with many special touches. The children all helped move

A new schoolhouse built by the school children's fathers and decorated by their mothers.

the desks and books and other small items from the old schoolhouse to the new one.

It was not the government that built and paid for the new schoolhouse. It was not the taxpayers, either. It was the families of the children who wanted a safer place for their children to go to school.

That is the Amish way.

School prayer

One afternoon, I was visiting an Amish friend of mine named Gideon. We were talking about world happenings and I shared with him that our children are not allowed to pray in school. This really bothered Gideon, and he shook his head in disbelief.

A few days later, I brought some folks on a tour to Gideon's furniture-making shop and he called me aside and told me he had something to tell me. He said, "Susan, there are about one thousand one-room Amish schoolhouses in the United States. Each schoolhouse has approximately thirty-two children inside of them. Every single day, our children pray aloud and sing praises to God. I want you to know there are at least thirty-two thousand children praying and worshiping God in school every day."

Meeting a rocket scientist

Amish children study the basic subjects such as reading, writing, and arithmetic in school. One subject they usually do not learn is science.

One day, a woman who worked at NASA was on my tour. She was part of a team that helped send a crew to the moon. I was excited to share this with some of the Amish children on my tour. Our first stop was at a local Amish bakery. Eli, who was twelve years old, loved to greet and talk to our tour guests.

I introduced Eli to my tour guest and said, "Eli, this is Dana. Dana is a rocket scientist. She helped send a man to the moon!"

Eli's eyes became as round as quarters, and he replied, "What? A man went to the moon?"

And Dana, my tour guest, answered back, "Yes!"

Eli looked right at her and asked, "Did he come back?" We could not help but smile and hug our sweet innocent Eli and answer his profoundly serious question.

"Yes, Eli," we assured him, "they came back!"

FIVE

DATING, SINGINGS, AND WEDDINGS

Amish teenagers

Formal education in an Amish school ends around age fourteen, but life education is just beginning. Boys will often begin apprenticing, usually with their fathers. They will learn such trades as furniture-making, roofing, housebuilding, and of course farming. All the money a boy earns goes to his parents until he is twenty-one, unless he marries young. His parents may give him an allowance or spending money, but most of the money he earns goes toward his family's household expenses. When the young man is ready to marry, his parents often will have tucked some of that money away to help him buy his first house or land.

Amish girls learn to sew and quilt. They contribute to the running of the homestead by cleaning, cooking, doing the laundry, and taking care of younger siblings. Some single young Amish women in our community are permitted to clean for English women, and others might work in an Amish-owned business. Some of the young women will be teachers.

I was asked by an Amish friend to pick up three schoolteachers and take them home. Their normal driver was sick, so they needed a replacement. I picked up each young teacher from her schoolhouse. To see each girl close her school's door and head to the car dressed in her blue or purple dress, heavy brown bonnet, and black cape, with a smile spread across her face, made my heart melt, and I felt as though I had stepped into a book written in the 1800s. The innocent beauty of the young Amish women never ceases to amaze me, even though I am around them daily.

The teachers carried lunch pails and black bags filled with school papers. Once they were all seated in the back seat of my car, they began chattering, and I was tickled that it was in English. The girls were sixteen, seventeen, and eighteen years of age. They talked about the wedding they had just attended, and the singing to be held the next Sunday at Henry and Leah's. They talked about what boys had been teasing them and what valentines they were making and for whom. They were teachers, but once in my car they became typical teenage girls.

The Maude

I sat down in my favorite handmade rocker in the corner of the Byler's living room, right next to Mamm's treadle sewing machine. My belly was warm and full, as we had just finished a lovely dinner of haystacks (an Amish favorite), with pineapple rings and homemade caramel sauce for dessert! Mamm lit the oil lamp, as it was just starting to get dark. Lydia and Sarah were clearing the table, little Ella was sweeping the floor, and the boys went out to milk the cows.

"Susan, do you know what a *Maude* is?" Mamm asked me.

"A Maude?" I questioned. "Is that an Amish word?"

"Yes," she replied. "It actually means 'maid' in your language. In our community, when a woman has a new baby, a younger girl about the age of fifteen or sixteen will often be sent to the mother's home to help. She will take care of the house, cook meals, and if there are other young children in the home, the Maude will help take care of them. This is so the new mother can have time to rest and bond with her newborn."

"Oh, that's such a great idea!" I exclaimed. I could not help but think back to when I had my second child, with a toddler already at home. How amazing it would have been to have a helper, mainly to get some extra sleep! "Does the Maude get paid?" I asked.

"No," Mamm continued. "The Maude is usually a niece or cousin of the new mother or a girl in the same church district. She is sent out of love to help and would not expect to be paid. Someday she will want the same help in return."

Lydia finished clearing the table, came into the living room, and sat down in the rocker next to mine. "Susan, I'm going to be a Maude to my aunt Rebecca this week. She just had a sweet baby boy. We were hoping you could drive me there tonight. I still need to finish the dishes and pack my suitcase, so if you don't mind staying awhile, I'll let you know when I'm ready."

"Lydia, is it typical for the Maude to spend the night?" I asked.

"Oh yes, the teenage girl will usually stay for a week, and then make day trips for a week after that. I will be at Aunt Rebecca's home for twelve days, because she has three other children under the age of six. She needs lots of help, Susan!" Lydia said with a giggle.

"Being a Maude is not just helpful for the new mother," Mamm explained. "It's also helpful for the young helper. Lydia will gain valuable experience, learning how to run a household on her own, being responsible to feed her family, and learning to take care of small children."

Many times, when I learn of the ways the Amish live life, I think to myself, Wow, why don't we do this in our society? This is brilliant! This was one of those times.

Sixteenth birthday

When Amish boys and girls reach the age of sixteen, three significant things happen in their lives. First, boys get their very own horse and buggy, and girls get their very own bedroom, and often a new bed.

Second, both boys and girls go through something called Rumspringa. *Rumspringa* means "running around," and in our community, Rumspringa is not such a wild time as many people are led to believe. It's more of a time when the Amish youth can have a few more freedoms than they will once they are baptized and join the church. It's a time to socialize and have fun. Rumspringa usually lasts a few years in our community; it ends when the young person is ready to be baptized into the church. Young women generally get baptized around the age of eighteen or nineteen, and young men around age nineteen or twenty. Usually Rumspringa ends when the youth are ready to settle down and be married.

Third, when Amish youth turn sixteen, they are invited to a singing. A singing is held every Sunday evening in our Amish community. One of the homes that hosted church will also host a singing for the youth. Young people gather and sit at a long table with benches on either side of the table. Boys sit on one side of the table and girls sit on the other side. They each bring a songbook with them to the singing. Girls call out a number from the songbook that they'd like to sing, and boys lead the song. The singing lasts about an hour. Afterwards, the youth have a meal together and then break off into groups of friends. This is a time for socializing. Boys usually spend time together with other boys, and girls spend time together with other girls. Friendships are formed that will last a lifetime.

Later in the evening, everyone gathers back at the singing house, and a boy may choose a girl to go on a buggy ride home from the singing. Sunday night is courting night in our Amish community. This buggy ride home is the only date that a boy and girl are permitted to go on. Amish youth in our community are not allowed to go to the movies, or out to eat in a restaurant, or bowling, or any other activity that many of our English teenagers enjoy. Usually, the youth don't start dating until they are eighteen years of age. They like to have time to make friends and enjoy those friendships before a courtship occurs.

Courting usually takes about two years. During this time of courtship, the couple are still only permitted to see each other on Sundays unless there is a wedding or another special event. Therefore, Amish youth love attending weddings. It's an extra opportunity to be with friends and one's sweetheart!

Rumspringa boys. PHOTO BY DIANNE GARRETT, USED WITH PERMISSION.

Weddings

In our community, Amish weddings are typically held on Tuesdays and Thursdays from October (after the last harvest) until March (before the first planting). Weddings start in the morning at nine sharp and usually go until midnight. It's fun to see buggy after buggy clip-clopping along the back roads of our Amish country filled with young men and women dressed in their finest church suits and dresses. Oh, the excitement!

All Amish couples keep their engagement a secret from everyone except their closest relatives until they are "published"—when the bishop makes an announcement in church that the couple will be married. This happens just two weeks before the wedding date, and after it does, the entire church congregation helps prepare for the wedding.

Amish benches lined up for a wedding. The chairs are for the bride and groom and their wedding party. PHOTO BY JAN SUMNER, USED WITH PERMISSION.

The wedding is hosted by the bride's parents. Actually, the wedding itself is usually held at a neighbor's home, with the reception at the home of the bride's parents. Friends, family, and church members come to the house and start cleaning and preparing for the wedding and reception. This includes fresh paint, new curtains, maybe even an extra addition built onto the house, which will end up hosting about 300–350 guests. There is shopping to do, personal invitations to be made, a seating chart to create (which singles will be matched with each other?), food to be made, and so on.

Days before the wedding, the women gather to help the family cook, because there are three meals served at an Amish wedding: a noon meal, an evening meal, and then a midnight meal for those helping clean up after the wedding. The women make pies and puddings, cookies, chicken, stuffing, salads, meatloaf, and so many other delicious foods. Even the men help cook! Men also remove most of the furniture from the first floor of the house, put it in the barn, and replace the furniture with rows and rows of benches and tables.

It takes a community to make the wedding work, but if there is anything the Amish do well, it is help one another. My Amish friend says, "Susan, when we help our friends and neighbors, we do so knowing that one day it will be our turn to need a helping hand. We do it because God commands us to love one another, and we do it with glad hearts. We love by serving."

A wedding starts with a church service, usually held at a neighbor's home or in one of their outbuildings. All the furniture or equipment is removed and replaced with rows of benches. Men sit on the right, women on the left, from oldest to youngest. The older children (only those who are close to the wedding couple are invited to a wedding) sit in the back. Two rows of chairs face each other in the middle of the rows of benches. Those are for the wedding party. The wedding ceremony is an ordinary church service, with singing and preaching. At the end of the service, the couple will say their vows.

The wedding reception is held at the home of the bride's parents. After most of the furniture is removed from every room except the bride's bedroom, benches and tables are placed all throughout the house. There is a head table for the wedding couple and their side sitters (equivalent to our maid of honor and best man or wedding party). This table is decorated with the bride's finest china that she has collected her entire life. Usually, as small girls, Amish girls choose a color—pink or blue (sometimes green or lavender)—and on every special occasion they will be given a piece of china in their color. When they are ready to be married, this is the china that will be used on their wedding day, and after marriage it will be displayed in their home as decoration.

Every couple has favor cards made for their wedding with their names and a sweet saying. These will be given to guests, and are especially treasured by the young guests, who take them home and hang them above their dressers as a souvenir.

The bride and groom wear special wedding outfits. Women in our community usually wear royal blue for their wedding dress. For the bride, it will be the last time she wears a black Kapp and a white apron (these are only worn by single women, and only on Sundays). As a married woman, she will switch to a white Kapp and a colored apron.

Wedding receptions include lots of eating and singing, laughing, and mingling. Men usually gather outside to smoke cigars or pipes while the women gather inside the house.

When the wedding of a young local Amish couple was announced, I took my friend Ella, who had just turned sixteen, and her mama all throughout New Wilmington on a hunt for a new black cap and fabric for a new dress

Traditional wedding attire for an Amish bride and groom in Lawrence County. After Amish women marry, they switch to a colored apron and white Kapp for church.

141

The fancy wedding table of an Amish bride and groom. The wedding cake is made by the bride's family. This table also includes gelatin salads in fancy containers and candy favors for the wedding party. PHOTOS BY JAN SUMNER, USED WITH PERMISSION.

and cape. Weddings are especially important and exciting social events for young Amish men and women. Although Amish youth are only permitted to visit with each other on Sundays, during wedding season they will see each other an extra day, sometimes even two. They might be matched with another young man or woman, so they want to look their best.

Each time Ella's mother would leave my car and go on an errand, Ella would giggle and share with me details about her plans for the wedding. Ella could not contain her excitement as she told me that there was a boy whom she thought would invite her to the table. (That is when a young man asks a young woman to sit across from him at the dinner table.)

A lot of matchmaking happens at Amish weddings. Side sitters will often try to seat a boy and girl whom they think would make a good match at the same table. Ella said that she might get a ride home in this boy's buggy after the wedding. I told her that I would be as excited as she was telling me about the wedding to hear everything that went on and whether she got her buggy ride home!

She said, "Oh, Susan, I probably won't tell you until it's steady!"

I replied, "Oh, Ella, you won't have to tell me, because I will be able to see it on your face!"

We both laughed, and softly and seriously, Ella said, "You're probably right." Then we both broke out in a fit of giggles!

Have you ever wondered what a grocery list for an Amish wedding looks like?

My Amish friend who had a daughter marry recently told me that the average cost for an Amish wedding is $6,000. Most of that money is for the food to feed all the guests. Three meals are served. The first two are for the guests, and the last meal, called a midnight meal, is for all the young people who stay to help clean up. That meal consists of pizza, candy, ice cream, and cake.

My friend's list looked like this:

1 gallon dried tea
1 case Maxwell House filter pack
    coffee
200 pounds chicken legs and thighs
4 whole chickens for gravy, stuffing,
    or noodles
75 pounds ground chuck
30 pounds bologna or turkey or ham
30 pounds Swiss cheese
15 pounds hot pepper cheese
15 pounds marble cheese
5 milk pails potatoes (4 fifty-
    pound bags)
1 bushel cabbage
5 heads lettuce
10 packages carrots
10 packages celery
6 bunches fresh parsley
5 pounds onions
1½ bushels apples for sauce
½ box oranges
15 pounds seedless grapes
2 gallons (16 cans) pineapple chunks
6 quarts canned peaches
40 loaves bread for stuffing (13
    dishpans)
25–30 loaves store-bought bread
    (for table)
2 large dishpans pie crumbs
9 pans date pudding
8 quarts strawberry jam
1 case oleo (10 pounds for table)
1 gallon cooking oil
1½ cases eggs

6 pounds pear tapioca
6 pounds macaroni
1 case whipped topping
4 pounds nuts
8 pounds dates
8 boxes corn flakes
15 boxes white crackers (10 for
    meatloaf, 5 for chicken)
8 pounds navy beans or 22 pounds
    frozen peas
3 pounds wieners (for beans)
5–8 boxes Velveeta
10 cans cream of mushroom soup
1 pail frosting
1 (5-pound) bag noodles
3–4 pounds turkey ham for noodles
    (cubed)
2 gallons salad dressing
6 large bottles ketchup
2 large bottles mustard
1 large can Lawry's seasoned salt
2 cans chicken base
10 pounds salt
1 pound black pepper
100 pounds bread flour
100 pounds white sugar
50 pounds pastry flour
25 pounds brown sugar
5 pounds Clear Jel (thickener for
    cherry pies)
20 cakes
40 pumpkin pies
20 cherry pies
10 raspberry or raisin pies

1 roll plastic table cover	120 candy bars
1 (8-roll) package paper towels	10 pounds candy
2 (12-count) packs toilet paper	4 boxes cigars
2 cans nonstick spray	6 bags potato chips
3–5 boxes wide aluminum foil	3 pails ice cream
3 boxes plastic wrap	6 (12-slice) pizzas
50 gallons kerosene	8 (2-liter) bottles soft drink
8 oil stoves and ovens	10 gallons milk
8–10 alpaca stoves	

There you have it!

Good Apple Girls

When Amish young folks date, the boy chooses a girl. A girl would never even acknowledge that she is interested in a boy, let alone ask a boy on a date. (Some of the Amish teenagers tell me that she would get an awfully bad reputation if it was known that she liked a boy!) It is left up to the boys to pick a girl.

So, you see, there are some young women who are never chosen to go on a date. These are called "Good Apple Girls." Amish friends told me a story that explains the name: Girls are like apples, and sometimes the sweetest and best apples are at the very top of the apple tree. It takes an extraordinarily strong and special man to climb to the top of that tree and choose one of those apples, and it is rare to find a man who is willing to take that chance. So some women, just like those apples, may be extremely sweet and good, but they still go unpicked. Those are the Good Apple Girls.

That is what our Amish friends call the women who never marry. They belong to a sort of club, and the community will make sure they are loved and supported. Often, they will live either with their parents or in a small house built behind a brother's home. They will live most of their lives by themselves, although in the Amish community nobody is ever alone. They will still be surrounded by many nieces and nephews, friends, and family. These Good Apple Girls even meet with each other and travel or go to other Amish communities for adventures. Sometimes the married women will have them over for a meal and games or a scavenger hunt to make sure they are not forgotten and left alone.

In our community, it was big news when a Good Apple Girl who had been single for about thirty years got picked! She was going to be married to David, a farmer who had lost his wife about two years earlier. He had five children. Two of his oldest sons were married, and he had three still at home. His wife died on their youngest child's sixth birthday. David and Sarah attended the same church, and after a few months of courting, David asked Sarah to be his wife and stepmother to his children. Sarah said yes!

David and Sarah had a traditional wedding and reception because Sarah had never been married.

I'm sure David was devastated when his wife passed away, and I imagine that Sarah thought she would never find love. God brought them together and created a brand-new family. I just love how God works things out, and I really love the fact that we should never, ever give up hoping.

Sunflower girl

Katie was married to her sweetheart at the age of nineteen. They bought a little house and some land and were so excited to begin their life together and create a family. Three months after the wedding, Katie's husband passed away unexpectedly. He was so young, and so full of life. Katie now had a decision to make. She could stay at the little house that she and her husband made into a home, or she could move back in with her parents.

Katie decided to stay in her little house and support herself as much as she could, so she created bouquets of flowers to sell at the local auction house.

But that is not the end of the story, because God is so much greater than that. Katie met a young Amish man from another Amish community who also lost his spouse at an incredibly early age. Johnny's young wife died of a heart attack at the age of twenty-three, along with the baby she was carrying. Johnny had a little one-year-old already at home. He was heartbroken and grieved tremendously. How was he going to raise a daughter without his wife? Along came sweet Katie with her sunflowers. Johnny and Katie fell in love through corresponding and, like Katie's lovely flowers, their love bloomed and blossomed. Johnny met Katie in person, and their love became stronger. He soon asked Katie to be his bride. They were married, and Katie sold her little house and moved to be with Johnny and his little girl. God gave each of them another opportunity for love and to grow a beautiful family together. Oh, God, you are so amazing!

Katie the sunflower girl drives a buggy of flowers to the auction.

SIX

FUNERALS AND BLESSINGS

WHEN SOMEONE in the Amish community dies, the members of the church district gather to help with the funeral. The moment a person dies, even if it's in the middle of the night, a neighbor will be summoned. That neighbor will tell their next-door neighbor, and word of mouth will continue until the entire church district is made aware of the passing. Everyone gathers at the deceased person's home, which is also where the viewing and funeral will take place. In our community, the Amish have their own cemeteries.

Lots are chosen to determine the four men who will dig the grave. Other men will make the pine box to be used as the coffin. Some men will prepare the bed (where the body lies during the wake) and others will get the barn ready for the many horses and guests that will arrive. Women will cook, clean, and bake and be there to comfort the grieving family.

An Amish man and woman walk home from a funeral. PHOTO BY SARA KLINE, USED WITH PERMISSION.

A wooden board made to resemble a bed is set up in the bedroom of the deceased. The body of the deceased will be laid out on the board, and many visitors will come to the house to pay their respects. The viewing is always the day after the death, even if it's a holiday. The burial will be on the third day. Funerals are very somber occasions, with little talking.

My Amish friend Mary allowed me to tag along on a visit to a sweet woman who had lost her husband suddenly in a farming accident. When I arrived at Mary's house, she was just adding some sprinkles to a beautiful cake that she had made for the woman and her children.

"Susan, there's a box filled with groceries on the back porch," she said. "David will help carry it to your car. Next to the box is a guest-book and pen. I thought she would like to keep a guestbook of all her visitors that she will have this year. Would you mind grabbing that?"

I picked up the pen and guestbook, and David followed me out to my car with the box of groceries. Mary followed, dressed in her *Medlyn* and *Iver Kapp* (cape and traveling bonnet) and carrying her cake.

As we drove to the widow's home, Mary explained that when someone dies, especially unexpectedly or when the person is young, the Amish community will send members to visit that grieving family for about a year so that the family will not be alone in their grief. "Each church district will take a turn," said Mary. "So each family in my church district will choose a day or evening to visit the grieving family, and most will bring a special treat, a meal or something they might need, like this box of groceries. Susan," Mary continued, "you might not know this, but I lost my first child when he was two years old."

Oh, my heart just sank when she said those words. "What happened, Mary?" I asked.

As her eyes welled up, Mary looked out the window and replied, "Aaron drowned in a neighbor's pond. I was doing the laundry and he was playing with the basket of clothespins. I went inside to get another basket, came back, and he was gone."

My tears could not be contained as I reached over and squeezed Mary's hand.

"Susan," she continued, "I did not want to see anyone during the days after the funeral. Not my mother or my sisters or even my own husband. But they would not leave me alone. They would take turns sitting next to my bed hour after hour, day after day. Sometimes they would talk. Sometimes they would sing. Sometimes they would just sit in silence. They would have to feed me. I could not even find the strength to feed myself. They would wipe away my tears that were like a dripping faucet in need of repair. It took a while, but eventually I could get dressed and make it out to our living room and sit in a rocking chair. And then one day our bishop was visiting, and his wife told me a funny story and I actually laughed. It was the first time I had laughed in an awfully long time. It was then that I knew I was going to be able to go on."

Mary continued, "I don't know if I would have made it without those friends and neighbors who never gave up on me. That is why I know it is important to be there for others in need. 'Do unto others that you would have done unto you.' We learn the golden rule in school, when we are young, and we try to live our lives by that rule as we grow old."

My heart was filled with awe and wonder. These people have touched my soul and changed the way I think and live. I pray that I can also remember the golden rule and live more like Mary and my Amish friends.

Saturdays are usually my busiest days touring Amish country. I often have tours from eight in the morning until six in the evening. One Saturday, my last tour cancelled, so I was able to finish around four.

One of the stops on my tour is Anna's Bakery. Anna is an Amish woman with seven children who sells donuts and other scrumptious baked goods right out of the basement of her home. She usually wakes up between three and four on Saturday mornings to begin making donuts. Guests arrive as early as seven to find trays full of just-made and still warm Amish donuts! On Saturdays, Anna and her children make donuts and wait on customers all day long. When my last tour arrives, there are still smiles on their faces as they greet my guests. They are cleaning up from the day's work and I can see the tiredness in their eyes and on their bodies as the day comes to an end.

This particular Saturday I noticed that Anna had many donuts left over, which is very unusual. She said, "Susan, I would like to ask a favor of you."

"Anything, friend!" I replied.

"There are two families I know who would be blessed if we sent what is left to them. One is a widow with six children at home. She does not have much. I think they would be excited to have some donuts and other baked goods. The second family has nine sons under the age of fourteen. They will surely be happy to receive some unexpected treats this evening."

"Anna, I would be honored to pass these blessings onto these families."

I was not yet finished with my last tour, so I asked the group if they would like to come along and deliver the goodies to these two Amish families. They felt equally honored.

We made our way up to the first long driveway. The first delivery was to Elizabeth Byler, the widow with six children. As we pulled up toward the house, I did not see anybody around, so I honked my horn. Soon little barefooted boys and girls came running around the house, followed by Elizabeth.

"Hello, Susan! It is good to see you!" said Elizabeth.

I told her that it was even better to see me with the boxes of donuts and pies and breads that Jake and Anna had sent for her!

She laughed and said, "Oh, Susan, these couldn't have come at a better time. We were canning all day, and I just haven't had time to fix supper. We will eat these donuts with our fresh peaches."

Elizabeth lost her husband Seth in a sawmill accident. She was pregnant with her sixth child at the time. I came to know her through a story that I had written about her a few years earlier. I was blessed to be able to help Elizabeth and her family after her husband's death.

I asked how she was getting along, and she smiled wearily. "We are doing the best we can, considering our circumstances." She told me of her oldest daughter, who was now, at fifteen, working at a greenhouse to bring in money, and her fourteen-year-old son working a job to help with the family also . . . but he was planning to return to school that week.

Oh, it just tugged at my heartstrings. I wanted to do more to help. I gave Elizabeth my business card with my phone number and told her to call me if she needed a ride or if there was any other way I could help. As I talked, we delivered the boxes of baked goods into the hands of several hungry children! They were so happy and oh so grateful.

The next delivery was to the family with nine sons. I had never met them before. As I pulled into their driveway, there were indeed nine little boys in denim trousers and blue shirts playing barefoot in the yard. Again, it warmed my heart to see the excitement of the unexpected blessing. The mama sat right down in the middle of the yard with her boys surrounding her as she passed out donuts to each of them. She waved and said, "Please tell Jake and Anna thank you, and thank you too, Susan, for the special delivery."

Jake and Anna were blessed to be able to share in their blessings. I was blessed to be able to pass them on. My tour guests were blessed to see the beautiful Amish families, and of course the recipients of the donuts and sweets were also blessed.

God is so good. If God has blessed you, please pass the blessings on to someone in need. Do not stop. Do not stop being kind and loving and sharing with what God has given you. Do all the good you can to all the people you can with all that God has given you.

PHOTOS BY BRIAN SCHMITT, USED WITH PERMISSION.

SEVEN

HOLIDAYS

I OFTEN get asked if the Amish celebrate holidays. My answer is yes, they celebrate most of the holidays that we celebrate, and even have a few holidays of their own.

Christmas

The Amish celebrate Christmas much as we do, but in a much less commercialized way. Christmas is about the birth of Christ, and the celebrations are to honor him. The Amish have no Christmas trees, no lights, and no Santa Claus. The children will often have a Christmas program at school, where they will sing Christmas songs and sometimes even make a nativity.

The Amish do exchange Christmas gifts. Children will receive a puzzle or game or a set of books. The older girls may receive something for their kitchen or home that they will put in their hope chest, and the boys might get a new gun or knife or special tool. They make homemade candy and other sweets. My friend wraps a box of presents for each of her children and places them on top of her china cupboard so the children can see. She will say, "If you want that Christmas gift, you must behave." My friend said that her children, just like English children, get extremely excited for Christmas. On Christmas morning, they get stockings with candy and small toys and treats.

The Amish also love sending and receiving Christmas cards. Often, they will string their cards in their homes as decorations.

Oh, what fun it is to shop for Christmas with a group of Amish women! Deer antler picture frames with handmade signs inside (the Amish do not have photographs) that say "To my sweetheart" and the couple's names written within two connecting hearts. A new muzzleloader for Lydia's husband, a gun safe for Jacob. Teena repaired and repainted an old antique John Deere tractor replica for her husband Andy. A mug with a pretty cardinal for Grandma, and games and puzzles for the children.

Christmas is such a sweet, fun time for Amish families. They are baking, and writing Christmas cards, and preparing their homes for their many family gatherings. The love of Christ abounds, and they make sure everyone is remembered and thought of this season.

It is different from our Christmas. No Santa Claus, no Christmas tree, and no stacks of gifts. But there is love, oh, there is so much love!

Let's make our Christmas about love too, my friends. Being together with family. Loving one another. Prepare your hearts. Ask Christ to fill those hearts with his love, and then go and pour it out to everyone you see and know.

On a visit just before Christmas with my favorite Amish family, we sat around the family table playing spoons together. The home was so cozy and warm, lit by oil lamp. It smelled heavenly from the apples that had been baking in the oven.

The boys brought out their coyote pelt to show us, as well as several books about birds and sea creatures that they had been looking at. Datt told stories about his hunting trip. He had left at four-thirty in the morning with two of his brothers. No luck with the big buck, but his eldest brother did snag a doe. I asked him if there was competition among his brothers, and his wife laughed aloud, knowing just how competitive the five boys . . . er . . . grown men are with each other.

The children showed us all their Christmas cards, which hung on three different strings that stretched across the living room. By the time Christmas Day came, there would be no room left on those strings and the room would be filled to the brim with Christmas love written on those pretty cards.

On top of the china cupboard sat three boxes wrapped in Christmas paper. Each child's gift was displayed, and Mamm said that they were set there as reminders for the children to be extra good so they could receive those presents on Christmas morning.

The children shared the poems that they would recite for their school Christmas program and shared with us the songs they would sing: "Joy to the World" and "Away in the Manger."

It was evident that this family knew the true meaning of Christmas, and they helped me remember the importance of keeping it simple. Do not let the decorating and baking and shopping keep you from the real reason that we celebrate the season. Christ was born!

Away in the manger, no crib for a bed,
the little Lord Jesus laid down his sweet head.
The stars in the sky looked down where he lay,
the little Lord Jesus asleep in the hay.

Old Christmas

Our Amish friends also celebrate Old Christmas, or Alt Chrischdaag. Old Christmas occurs each January 6 and is still widely observed as a holiday by many Plain folks, who commemorate the Epiphany with rest and fasting. The Epiphany, traditionally, is the day in which the wise men brought gifts to Jesus. However, January 6 is called Old Christmas because in 1582, Pope Gregory XIII deleted ten days from the calendar to realign it with the seasons of the year, thus technically moving Christmas from December 25 to January 6.

After a morning of rest and fasting, the Old Order Amish in Lawrence County often enjoy a big meal surrounded by family. My Amish friends tell me that Christmas Day is usually celebrated with local family so they don't have to call English "drivers" away from their homes to drive faraway family to their Christmas celebrations, but on Old Christmas, they often get together with faraway family and celebrate Christmas together with large meals, gifts, and family fun.

Valentine's Day

Do our Amish friends celebrate Valentine's Day? They sure do! Young dating couples usually buy each other Amish-made ceramic valentine hearts in their favorite color, and they fill them with their own home-made candy. My friends Linda and Emma bought their boyfriends ceramic hearts hand-painted and stenciled with each of their names on them. Another bought her boyfriend a set of coasters with a beautiful buck on each one. She was so excited to make a basket to put all his special presents in. They also make beautiful handmade cards to give to friends and loved ones. They are very romantic and sentimental!

Easter

Good Friday is a day of reflection and fasting for our Amish friends. The adults fast and pray until noon. Businesses are closed, and work stops for the day.

No Easter bunny comes on Easter with baskets full of sweets, but Amish children often dye eggs and hide them for the smaller children on Easter Sunday. The children bring little handmade baskets home from school and display them in the family's living room. Amish families focus on the true meaning of Easter, that Christ died on the cross and rose from the dead.

Ascension Day

Our Amish friends celebrate a holiday that many of us do not, called Ascension Day. Ascension Day celebrates the day that Jesus went up to heaven after being resurrected on Easter Sunday. It is forty days after

PHOTO BY DENISE GUTHRIE, USED WITH PERMISSION.

Easter Sunday and is always on a Thursday. Amish friends and families often go fishing and then have a cookout—sometimes a fish fry with the fish they caught. All Amish children have a day off school, and many Amish stores close on this day.

Fourth of July

Many Amish will watch July 4 fireworks from their homes or a nearby field, but they wouldn't attend a public event such as a parade or fireworks gathering.

One day my friend Levi said to me, "Susan, do you know why you will never see an American flag on an Amish barn or home?"

I told him that I did not know why.

"Because our home is not anywhere here on earth. If this country would not allow us to live and worship freely the way we choose to live and worship, then we Amish would move to another country," he told me. "Our loyalties are to a home in heaven."

Thanksgiving

Thanksgiving does not seem to be celebrated in a big way in our Amish community. Perhaps that's because our Amish friends give thanks every day for God's many blessings, and family gatherings happen often in their community. This is a Thanksgiving prayer that my Amish friend Lizzie gave to me for my Thanksgiving dinner. She said that her husband Amos often prays this aloud to their children.

> Thank you, Lord, for this bountiful harvest.
> Lord, when I have food,
> help me to remember the hungry;
> when I have work,
> help me to remember the jobless;
> when I have a home,
> help me to remember the homeless.
> When I am without pain,
> help me to remember those who are suffering.
> And remembering,
> help me to not feel complacent.
> Help me to feel compassion
> and to be concerned enough to help.
> Not just by my words, but by my actions.
> We take so much for granted.
> Amen.

EIGHT

AMISH DAILY LIFE
AND STORIES

Visits

One of my favorite things about having Amish friends is that they always have time for a visit. Married women do not work outside the home, and although they work extremely hard inside the home, they always are available to spend time together in conversation. "Susan, how are you? Come sit down and chat awhile. How is your granddaughter? Tell me what is going on with the Tavern. Did you hear about Eli?"

My mom tells me this is also how it used to be for her generation. We could learn so much from our older generation and our Amish friends. When is the last time you just went for a visit? When is the last time you sat on the porch with a friend and just talked with one

A porch is a place for Amish friends and neighbors to visit with one another.

another? What would you do if your doorbell rang and you were not expecting anyone?

If we all turned off our phones, televisions, and computers and talked to each other more, we might realize that we have a lot more in common with each other than we are often led to believe.

Technology

An Amish friend of mine shared this story with me, and it reminds me of how much technology makes our lives different. Has it made life better? Perhaps, but has it also caused us to lose touch with each other?

I had spent an hour in the bank with my dad, as he had to transfer some money. I couldn't resist myself and asked . . . "Dad, why don't we activate your Internet banking?" [Note: This story is from an Amish friend, but isn't about the Amish themselves!]

"Why would I do that?" he asked.

"Well, then you won't have to spend an hour here for things like transfer. You could even do your shopping online. Everything will be so easy!"

I was so excited about initiating him into the world of Internet banking.

He asked, "If I do that, I won't have to step out of the house?"

"Yes, yes!" I said. I told him how even groceries can be delivered at the door now, and how companies like Amazon deliver everything.

His answer left me tongue-tied.

He said, "Since I entered this bank today, I have met four of my friends, and I have chatted awhile with the staff, who know me very well by now. You know I am alone . . . this is the company that I

PHOTO BY BRIAN SCHMITT, USED WITH PERMISSION.

need. I like to get ready and come to the bank. I have enough time, it is the physical touch that I crave. Two years back I got sick, and the store owner from whom I buy fruits came to see me and sat by my bedside and cried. When your mom fell down while on her morning walk, our local grocer saw her and immediately got his car to rush her home, as he knows where I live. Would I have that human touch if everything became online? Why would I want everything delivered to me and be forced to interact with just my computer? I like to know the person that I'm dealing with and not just the 'seller.' It creates bonds of relationships. Does Amazon deliver all this as well?"

This story reminds us that technology is not life. Spend time with people, not with devices.

Horse and buggies

I asked my friend Gideon why the Amish drive horse and buggies instead of cars. Actually, I asked him, "Why are you allowed to drive in cars, but can't own or drive cars yourselves? Some people might think that's hypocritical!"

Gideon smacked his lips and shook his head at me (he often does that when I ask him questions). "Susan," he replied, "there are three reasons we Amish drive horse and buggies. First, it keeps us close to home and close to our families. You need to be surrounded by your family if you want to have the best life possible. Cars scatter people far away from each other, but horse and buggies keep our people close together, especially our families. You need your family nearby."

"The second reason," continued Gideon, "is it helps us have a slower pace of life. Susan, I noticed something about you English people. You always seem to be in a hurry, and you are always so busy. Amish people, we are not like that."

When I thought about it, I noticed that he was right. It seems to me that the Amish walk slower and talk slower. They don't ever seem to be in a hurry or rushed the way many of us are.

"Susan, you people need to slow down and enjoy the journey. Life goes by so quickly. Don't let it pass you by."

Oh my goodness, he is so right! I thought. This time I was the one to shake my head as I sighed and asked, "What's the third reason?"

"The third reason we Amish drive horse and buggy is because it helps us shop local. We believe in buying and selling as much as we can from each other so everybody in our community can make a living." Gideon continued, "Susan, don't spend your money at Walmart or Amazon—they have enough money. The small shop owners in your community need your money much more than the corporate people do. Now, do not get me wrong. There are times we need items that our small businesses do not have. That is when we will hire a driver to take us to those places, but for the most part, we shop locally and buy and sell from each other instead of those big stores. Horse and buggies keep us from traveling out of town to spend our money."

Truly, I was astonished. I thought that the Amish drove horse and buggies only because cars are modern. But with Gideon's help I realized there are many other good reasons that most of us just do not realize.

Business

I was talking to an Amish bishop one day about world events. I was telling him that there may come a day that the world will not use cash but only digital currency. I asked him this question: "Jake, if the Amish could no longer do business with English people, do you think the Amish could survive?"

He was very pensive. I could tell he was thinking, and it took him a while to answer. Finally, he said, "Susan, we'd have to make a shift. It would be very difficult. But I think we could do it."

We continued the conversation, and Jake told me how life has changed so much, even among the Amish. He said, "There's a joke we make. Grocery stores buy Amish produce and Amish produce growers buy their food from grocery stores." In other words, even the Amish don't eat only what they grow and harvest anymore. Jake continued, "Back in my grandparents' time, no one would ever travel just for pleasure. My grandparents lived just fifty miles from the ocean and never once saw it. They worked so hard just to survive. They didn't go to big stores like Walmart. Our young people have it too easy today. They have gotten soft, and they rely on the world an awful lot."

Jake continued to share about his own family. "My boys just butchered seventeen turkeys that we raised. My wife canned 111 quarts of turkey. That will last us a year. We raise our chickens for eggs and meat. My boys and I hunt, and venison stew is a family favorite. My boys can butcher a hog, and the girls know how to clean and preserve the fish we catch. We grow our own vegetables and some fruits. We grow hay to feed our seventeen horses. My wife and daughters bake fresh bread and a sweet dessert for us every day. How could a man ask for any more?"

He was quiet for a little while and then he said, "Susan, sometimes it's good to not have everything you want. God will provide everything you need. Work hard and trust the Lord to provide. That's what we will do."

Letter writing

When is the last time you handwrote a letter? Technology has taken over, and in today's world we communicate via text, phone, email, and computer. It seems that the distinctive touch of a handwritten letter has all but disappeared.

Our Amish friends communicate through word of mouth, face-to-face talk, and letter writing. Sending cards (often handmade) and writing letters is a quite common way of communicating among friends and family.

Boys and girls who are dating will often send each other handwritten letters on Wednesdays. They are permitted to see each other only on Sundays unless there is a wedding or other special event, so sending a love letter is a way for them to express their affection. How romantic it must be to receive a love letter once a week!

As I got ready to turn into the driveway of my Amish friend Linda, her teenage daughters Teena and Anna jumped out of the car and sprinted to the mailbox, each pushing the other to try to get there first.

"What is going on?" I laughed.

"Susie, it's Thursday," said Linda. "The girls are anxious to get their letters from their boyfriends!"

"Oh, love letters! I guess I would be pretty excited to get a love letter in the mail, too," I replied.

"You see," said Linda, "our girls and boys are only allowed to see each other on Sundays. When they are in love, seven days to see your sweetheart feels like an eternity. Usually, they will write each other letters and send them on a Wednesday so they will arrive on a Thursday. Most girls and boys will have a special chest they put the letters in after they are read over and over. Some might save those letters forever."

"Linda, do you still have your letters from David?" I asked with a wink and a smile.

"Yes, she does!" giggled her daughter Mary from the back seat of my car. "They are so gross, all gushy and mushy and filled with love words!" she squealed.

I could see the shy smile spread across Linda's face as her cheeks turned bright red.

"Someday you will be running to that mailbox hoping for one of those gushy and mushy love letters, Mary," I said.

"I'm never getting a boyfriend," replied Mary, "because a boyfriend turns into a husband, and having a husband takes too much work!"

"Mary," squealed Linda, "I think *you* are going to be the one that takes too much work!"

Amish children and teenagers like to write letters to a birthday twin—an Amish boy or girl who shares their birthday. After they discover (often through Amish directories or publications) that they share the same birthday, they begin writing letters to one another. I know several Amish girls in my community who have traveled great distances to meet their birthday twin after years of correspondence.

Another way the Amish communicate is through circle letters. Each person in a circle letter group writes a letter, which is added to a batch of previous letters from others in the group. The whole batch is then sent on to the next person on the list, who does the same, and so on. A circle letter is a way Amish people with common connections keep in touch. There are family circle letters and circle letters for people who share common interests or experiences such as stamp collecting or quilting. Circle letters are often advertised in Amish publications.

I do not know about your mailbox, but mine is filled with either bills or junk mail 99 percent of the time. When I get a handwritten note, letter, or card, my heart leaps! Sending a handwritten letter or card is a small thing to do for someone, yet it brings a great reward. The surprise, excitement, and gratitude that comes from receiving a handwritten card or letter is immeasurable!

Big news

It was big news in Amish country when Wally spotted a black bear in the woods behind his house.

"Datt went out to the barn to do the morning milking and he saw the bear tracks in the snow," exclaimed bright-eyed Harvey, Wally's five-year-old son.

PHOTO BY KOTENKO_A/ISTOCKPHOTO/GETTY

179

"It looked like the bear was trying to get into the barn, but Datt always keeps the barn door locked up tight at night," Wally's daughter Mary explained to me.

"There aren't usually bears around this part of Pennsylvania in February, right?" I asked.

"Not usually," Wally answered. "I've heard of bear sightings but never seen one in my whole life around here. I told the children that we usually would not have known if a bear was in our yard, because they only walk on the soles of their feet, so they do not leave distinct tracks. But they do leave tracks in the snow, and these were huge. I'll just bet it was about a five hundred-pound bear!"

"Well, what happened next?" I asked. This *was* exciting news!

Mary continued, "Datt ran into the house and got Johnny. He told him to get his gun just in case they encountered the bear."

"We were just getting ready to walk to school, and Datt didn't want us to walk our usual path through the woods, just in case that bear was still around," explained Harvey.

"So Datt and Johnny went outside with their guns and followed the tracks from our barn all the way through our back field. The bear had squeezed through our fence and went up to neighbor Eli Mast's field."

"Datt, show Susie what you have in your wallet," said Harvey with a proud smile lighting up that sweet little pink-cheeked face.

Wally pulled out his wallet from his front pants pocket and opened it up. Inside the wallet was a little plastic bag with a patch of black hair tucked inside.

"What on earth is that?" I asked.

Wally answered, "It's the bear's fur! I found it on the barbed wire of our fence. I saved it just in case nobody believes me when I tell them there was a bear in our backyard!"

Just then, big brother Johnny came around the corner with his arms out and shouted, "ROARRRRR!" The little ones screamed and ran behind Datt, grabbing on to his pant legs.

What joy to live a life where the biggest news of the week is finding bear tracks in your backyard.

A baby who changed everything

I went to visit a sweet Amish friend of mine named Emma who had just given birth to her fourth beautiful little girl, named Elizabeth. I arrived around nine in the morning, and I could not wait to see my friend and hold that precious baby in my arms. I sat down in my favorite rocking chair and the girls brought Elizabeth over to me. She was wrapped in pink from head to toe, her sweet little cheeks nearly as pink as her blanket. She had blue-gray eyes and a head full of dark hair.

PHOTO BY GUMMYBONE/ISTOCKPHOTO/GETTY IMAGES

When she looked up at me, I swear she smiled, and my heart swelled and a tear or two slid down my cheeks. You see, Elizabeth is an answer to prayer and a baby that has begun to heal a brokenhearted family. Let me tell you their story . . .

About a year earlier, Emma had carried another little girl in her womb. She worked all summer and fall while this precious child grew inside of her. For nine months Emma felt every kick, every jab, every roll, and then one day, two days before the baby was due, Emma felt no movement at all. She went to the doctor's office, but they could find no heartbeat. They had to deliver the baby by Cesarean section, and she was born without ever taking a breath—stillborn. Her birthday was also the day of her death.

They named their baby girl Mary. Emma's husband David brought their six other children to the hospital. Each child got a turn holding the baby, studying little Mary's features so they would never forget her. They spent the entire day together in that hospital room. The Amish are not allowed photographs, but the hospital staff inked the baby's

PHOTO BY STEPHANIE FREY/ISTOCKPHOTO/GETTY IMAGES

feet and created a beautiful keepsake of her footprints with her name and date of birth and death for the family to always have. David had the keepsake copied, and I was honored to receive one so I, too, could always remember baby Mary.

I went to visit Emma after she was discharged from the hospital. She was in her bed, dressed in a cap and a nightdress, her hair disheveled and eyes swollen. I sat next to her bed as she told me her story. I will never forget these words she spoke to me: "Susan, my breasts ache because they are supposed to be feeding my little girl. My arms ache because there is no baby for them to hold. My heart aches because she is not here with me." Emma was so filled with sadness that it made my own heart weep right along with hers.

But a year later, there was a new story to tell. A new baby, a beautiful gurgling healthy baby girl. And there was a much different feel to the room this time as I held little Lizzie.

Emma's eyes were filled with such joy as she shared with me the story of her birth. Emma's oldest daughter Sylvia sat on the floor cutting out pieces for a new dress, as there were a few weddings coming up in the next few weeks. Another daughter, Amy, was down in the basement doing laundry, since it was washday in our Amish village and there are lots of clothes to be washed for a family of nine! And then there was sweet little Leah.

Leah is three years old, and she is a wide-eyed, gap-toothed little ball of sunshine. Leah always carries a little ragdoll with her. It is her "baby," and she can usually be found diapering, or feeding, or changing that little baby's clothes all the while talking to me in Pennsylvania Dutch while I nod my head or say *ya* (yes) or *nee* (no) or sometimes "Oh, okay." Once in a while I'll ask the family to interpret, but most of the time my yas and nees and okays are enough for little Leah.

This visit was so very special because Leah now had a *real* baby to love and care for, and I knew beyond any doubt she was going to be a great big sister. This new baby was bringing hope and healing to this family that sure did need it.

We all have different stories; our lives are often filled with heartache, and many of us need hope and healing too. Oh, my friends, when the days are dark and your heart is filled with sadness or loneliness, remember: there was a baby who changed everything.

Rich in blessings

One day, my Amish friend Lydia and I were having lunch and talking about life and she said, "Susan, just think how rich we are. We have warm beds to sleep in each night. We have more food than we need, and we can fill our bellies whenever we are hungry. We have clothes to wear and fresh water to drink. We have a God who loves and cares for us, and perhaps our greatest blessing that God has given us is our family."

With tears in my eyes I replied, "Lydia, we are rich indeed." I could not help but think how much life is about our attitude and perspective. I am so grateful and thankful for the many, many blessings God has given me, and I sometimes feel as though I am the richest person in the world.

It is wonderful to take some time alone to go somewhere quiet, away from the everyday distractions of life, and think about how rich we really are. Take some time to reflect on your life—think about the many blessings God has given and ask yourself, "What is important to me?" When you strip away each layer of your life, I bet at the core you will find God and you will find other people. Does anything else really matter? God and people. We need God and we need each other!

Luke 10:27 says, "'Love the Lord your God with all your heart and with all your soul and with all your strength and with all your mind'; and, 'Love your neighbor as yourself.'" Love God. Love people. Truly, it is that simple. We just make it so complicated.

Gratitude

Gratitude can transform ordinary days into thanksgivings, it can turn routine tasks into joyful opportunities, and it changes struggles and hardships into blessings. Gratitude unlocks the fullness of life. It turns what we have into enough, and more. It turns denial into acceptance, chaos into order, and confusion to clarity. It can turn a meal into a feast, a house into a home, a stranger into a friend. Gratitude makes sense of our past, brings peace for today, and creates a vision for tomorrow.

When you encounter negativity and division from television and social media, do not let it control your thoughts! If you are frustrated about what is happening in the world, take some advice from our Amish friends.

While you cannot control the actions of others, you can control your own.

Today, you can choose to:

Be happy.
Work hard.
Love others.
Make a difference.
Inspire others and believe in them.
Raise your children with great values and principles.
Be the example.
Stay positive.
Pray.

Let's remembers the values of our faith: Love. Faithfulness. Christian community. Demonstrating care for others. Personal behavior and responsibility. Collective compassion. Focus on being your best and bringing out the best in others.

If we all do that, we all win.

When we put our problems in God's hands, God puts his peace in our hearts.

Encounters with God

A few years back, an Amish family lost their son in a farming accident. Jake was just sixteen. His family was absolutely devastated, but no one was more heartbroken than Jake's father Daniel. In their family, as in many other Amish families, the children would work right alongside their parents. Jake had been Daniel's right-hand man from the time he was old enough to walk. He followed his daddy around, learning how to milk the cows each morning at sunrise and each evening around sunset. He rode along on his daddy's plow behind the big workhorses as they cleared, plowed, fertilized, and planted fields of corn. If you saw Daniel, Jake was usually by his side. They were not only father and son but also best friends. Jake had just turned sixteen and had been working on his new buggy. Soon he would be going to Sunday singings and participating in all the youth activities. But God had other plans for Jake.

Daniel could barely function after the death of his son. The cows still needed milking, and the fields still needed to be plowed, but Daniel lost his will to do those things without his beloved son by his side. One morning he woke up, looked over at his wife, and said, "I can't do this anymore. I want to sell the farm and move away." His wife was heartbroken too, but she could not even think about moving away from her family and community, who had been there and continued to be there for her and Daniel to help them as they grieved.

On this day, Daniel made the decision that he was indeed going to sell the farm. As he was getting his horses hitched up to start the day's field work, a car pulled into the edge of his long gravel driveway. An English man got out of the car and walked toward Daniel, with a very unusual gait. Daniel wondered if the man was drunk. He stood with his horses and watched as the man came toward him, creating such a strange sight to see as he stumbled toward the barn. The man reached Daniel, and he seemed perfectly normal.

"Can I help you with something?" Daniel asked.

"Yes," the man replied, "do not sell your farm for at least one year."

Daniel was dumbfounded. It was as if that man had read his mind! How on earth could he possibly know what Daniel had been thinking that very morning? Daniel had never seen this man in his life. Daniel was so in shock over these words that he could not reply, but he did not need to, because before he could react, the man was gone.

That shook Daniel to his core. He felt so strange, and he could not believe what had happened. *Who was that man, and how did he know what I was thinking?* Daniel decided not to tell anybody about his encounter with the stranger. His family was already concerned about his mental health. He hitched up his team of horses and went out into the fields.

When Daniel finished plowing, he put Buster and Smoky, his two Belgian workhorses, back into the barn, and just when he came out, another English man's car pulled up to the edge of his driveway. The car stopped, and a man got out. He walked the same unsteady pattern

PHOTO BY DENISE GUTHERY, USED WITH PERMISSION.

all the way up the drive and approached the barn. He, too, said, "Don't sell your farm for at least one year."

This time Daniel got angry. *How does this man know I want to sell my farm, and what business is it of his? He has no idea that I just lost my son and what I am going through!* Daniel wanted to hit him, but the Amish are taught to be passive and not to fight. Just as with the first encounter, the man walked back to his car without Daniel replying.

By now, Daniel knew that something strange was going on. This was not a weird coincidence. He began to shake, and he started to cry. He walked up to his porch and sat down and put his head into his hands as he sobbed for his beloved son and the strange encounters he had just experienced.

Friends, this is a true story, and it's not over. Can you guess what happened next? A third car, a third stranger, a third walk up the gravel driveway, and the third exact statement: "Don't sell your farm for at least one year."

This time Daniel looked at the man through tear-soaked eyes and said, "Thank you." As the man walked back to his car, Daniel knew that he had encountered God not once, but three times that day.

Today, he still owns his farm, and although he still mourns the loss of Jake, Daniel knows that God is watching over him.

Daniel finished telling me this story by saying, "Susan, ask me what those men looked like."

So I asked him. "What did those men look like?"

"I have no idea," Daniel replied. "That day, after I had the three encounters, I could not tell you either. It is like God erased them from my memory. I remember their cars, their walks, and exactly what they said to me, but I have no idea who they were or what they looked like."

God finds ways to let us know that he is with us always. Tragedies still happen, but God will always be there in our midst when we need him most.

Stronger together

I have had several meals with a friend who is also a bishop in our Amish community. I love to listen to his words of wisdom. One evening after dinner we were talking about current world events. I told him that I believe Satan is trying to divide us and make us hate one another, when God has told us to love one another. Jake looked at me, smiled, and began to tell me a story:

"There was a father who had several sons who were forever quarreling among themselves. No words the father could say would make those sons stop fighting. He prayed that God would give him a way to show his sons that division is no good, neither among a family or a church nor a community or a nation. The father knew that discord would lead them to misfortune.

"One day, when the quarreling had been much stronger and louder than usual and each son was working around the farm with anger in his heart and a poor attitude, the farmer asked one of his sons to bring him a bundle of sticks. He called all his boys together and handed each one a stick. 'Sons,' the farmer said, 'I want you to try to break these sticks I have given you.' Each son easily broke the one stick that he was holding.

"Then the father gathered all the broken sticks together and he tied them into a bundle. 'Now, sons, I want you to break this bundle of sticks.' The oldest son puffed out his chest and tried to break the bundle in two, but it was easy to see that there was no way he or any of the other boys would be able to break that bundle of sticks.

"'My sons,' said the father, 'do you not see how certain it is that if you agree with each other and help each other, it will be impossible for your enemies to injure you? But if you are divided among yourselves, you will be no stronger than a single stick in that bundle.'

"You see, Susan," said my bishop friend, "there is strength in unity. Our enemies will try to divide us, but it is important for us to stick together as one. We Amish believe in unity over individualism because of that very reason. We are stronger together."

If only our world would understand this lesson taught by our Amish friends. "Dear children, let's not merely say that we love each other; let us show the truth by our actions" (1 John 3:18 NLT).

The power of forgiveness

I was shopping at an Amish bookstore and I picked up a book called *Bedenklich Happenings* (*bedenklich* means "unusual" in Pennsylvania Dutch). It is filled with stories, poems, and articles collected by a man named Levi Fisher. As I was reading, I came across a story that was truly relevant to what is happening in today's world.

Our hearts are like this field. We can grow kindness or selfishness, bitterness or forgiveness, compassion, or indifference. What seeds will you plant? PHOTO BY BRIAN SCHMITT, USED WITH PERMISSION.

The story is about an Amish bishop who was not very well liked in his community. One night, a group of young men came to the bishop's house and climbed up onto his roof. The men began ripping shingles off and throwing them onto the ground. The young men were laughing, and the bishop heard them say, "This is payback for his always keeping his eyes on us and reprimanding us when we get out of line."

The bishop's wife was very frightened, and she asked her husband what they should do. The bishop told his wife to go to the kitchen and to begin cooking breakfast. "But it is the middle of the night!" she exclaimed.

"Yes," her husband replied, "but we have visitors. They are working hard, and we must show them that we love them."

The bishop's wife nodded with understanding. She went to the kitchen and started to prepare a meal for their visitors. The bishop got dressed, then he went downstairs, opened the door, and said to the young men, "Hello. You must be very hungry from working so hard. Please come inside and have something to eat. My wife has prepared a nice breakfast for you."

The men were so startled, they didn't know what to do.

"Hurry and come inside before it gets too cold."

The young men went inside and sat down at the kitchen table. The bishop's wife served them some eggs she had prepared, but the men were so shocked and filled with guilt that they couldn't eat. They lowered their heads, and the leader of the young men pushed his plate away and rose from the table. He went outside and the other men followed.

The bishop looked at his wife and smiled. Soon they heard loud noises coming from the roof. The young men were nailing the shingles back onto the roof.

Whom do you need to forgive today? I pray that God opens your heart and takes out the bitterness that you are holding on to and replaces it with mercy, grace, and forgiveness.

The most valuable things

My friend Paul and I often sit and have lengthy discussions in his living room. He and his wife Mary are dear friends of mine, and I am often invited for dinner in their home. Paul loves the Lord. When he was a young Amish boy, he left the Amish community and lived among the English for a time. After a few years he went back and was baptized into the Amish church and has lived Amish for sixty-five years now.

Paul said, "Susan, when I was a small boy, I wanted a pickup truck more than anything in the world. When I became a teenager, I still wanted that pickup truck. I thought English men wearing cowboy hats and driving a pickup truck were the coolest people in the entire world. So I left the Amish, bought a cowboy hat, and worked in a local restaurant until I saved up enough money to buy that pickup truck. I moved into an apartment above the restaurant, and it did not take me long to realize that all that money I was making at the restaurant went into paying bills. There was so little left over for me to enjoy the life I wanted to live. The thrill of owning that truck wore off, and I realized that having a family surrounding you with love and acceptance was so much better than anything you could own. I went back and asked for forgiveness from my parents and community and church, and I found it. I also found love and acceptance among my people, the Amish."

Paul continued, "People often say the life of the Amish is a hard life, but I've lived both lives, English and Amish, and in my opinion the life of an English person is much harder. You need to love God more than anything in this world, including a fancy new truck. When I was young, I did not realize that. I did not understand that everything comes from God, and I certainly did not understand that your family and community and church are far more valuable than anything money could buy."

Wise advice from a man who has lived both English and Amish.

"Blessed are the meek, for they shall inherit the earth"

One of the many wonderful biblical principles that I've seen the Amish live out is meekness. They are pacifists and are taught to "turn the other cheek" if wronged.

In a book entitled *History of the Patriarchs for the Young*, which is written for young Amish men and women and is sold in many Amish bookstores, there is a passage that asks,

> Are you meek, my dear reader? Can you bear to be pushed and struck, and not push and strike again? If anyone takes your place, can you ask him gently to let you have it, and if he will not, can you take another quietly? When people call you rude names, can you be gentle, and not call them rude names too?
>
> If you are meek, you can do all these things. God can make you very meek, my dear friend. Will you pray to God to make you meek, like Jesus?[2]

Psalm 37:11 says, "The meek will inherit the land and enjoy peace and prosperity."

Could it be that following biblical principles and living a humble and simple life modeled after Jesus Christ is what brings peace, joy, happiness, and even prosperity to these special people? In my experiences of living among them and befriending many of them, I would say the answer to this question is a definite yes. I have embraced many of their values, and in many ways I have learned to live a simpler way of life like the Amish, and it has brought these things to me. It is my

2   American Tract Society, *History of the Patriarchs for the Young* (New York: American Tract Society, 1858), 354–56.

prayer that this encounter with the lives and stories of the Amish will stir you to embrace a meaningful change in your life, too.

PHOTO BY BRIAN SCHMITT, USED WITH PERMISSION.

CONCLUSION

In the same way, let your light shine before others, that they
may see your good deeds and glorify your Father in heaven.
—*Matthew 5:16*

THE MORE I toured Amish country and the more I got to know
my Amish friends, the more I began to see how different their lives
were from mine, and the more I desired to live a simpler life like theirs.
In this world that is faster paced and busier than ever, it is easy to get
caught up in the feeling of needing to do increasingly more just to keep
up with everyone else.

I wanted my life to slow down. I wanted to become more at peace
and more mindful of my days. I watched my Amish friends and
learned how to slow down. I spent more time outdoors, enjoying
God's beautiful earth. I shut off my phone and I was able to turn

off the noises of the world. I began to set my alarm for five in the morning, and I would watch the sunrise each morning as I prayed. My days seemed to have so much more time in them, even though time had not changed. It was I who had changed. I thought of my Amish friends' homes that were plain and simple but so beautiful. I decluttered my home, and it is now so much easier to keep clean and organized.

My definition of success has changed significantly since getting to know the Amish community. I used to value money and nice things. Now I've come to realize that God, family and community are most important. I've learned to lead a life of humbleness, calmness and placidity. I've learned to slow down and enjoy the journey. I have changed my priorities in life accordingly. Living a life more pleasing to God and loving him is what is most important to me now. Each day I wake up with a heart filled with gratitude and thanksgiving, praising our Father in heaven for another day to glorify him.

I now spend more time with the people I love. In the past I would hardly ever have the time to sit down on a porch and visit with a friend or family member, but now I make the time. We need each other more than ever before. People are lonely. Social media has created a world where people stay in their houses even when they want to connect with others. Technology has taken over, and face-to-face talk has diminished. Instead, we communicate through text, phones, emails, and computers. We get depressed when we compare ourselves to others, forgetting that social media shows the (often exaggerated) highlights of people's lives.

Unplug. Write a letter to someone you love, and even better yet, go and visit. Take a dessert or casserole, fresh flowers, or something from your garden. Take your children to visit an elder. Teach them to love and respect our older generation. They need our smiles and our touches.

The Amish have taught me that people need each other more than technology. The days that I am happiest are the days that I am with people. I care less about making money and more about spending time with people I love.

I have found inspiration among the Amish that has changed my life in so many wonderful ways. It is my hope and prayer that you have been touched and inspired by the simple life of the Amish, and I hope that it helps make your life a better one, too.

With the love of the most amazing Creator and Savior of the world, Your friend Susan.

If you would like to read more stories about the simple life of the Amish, you can find me on Facebook at Simple Life in New Wilmington, Pa.

If you would like to take a Simple Life tour in New Wilmington, Pennsylvania, it would be my honor to show you the Amish community that I love so very much.

Visit my website at www.SimpleLifeTours.com.

"You are my sheep, the sheep of my pasture, and I am your God," declares the Sovereign LORD. —Ezekiel 34:31 NIV

"He has made everything beautiful in its time. He has also set eternity in the human heart; yet no one can fathom what God has done from beginning to end." —Ecclesiastes 3:11

ACKNOWLEDGMENTS

FIRST AND foremost, praises and thanks to Jesus Christ, my Savior for His showers of blessings throughout the writing of this book. He has truly made my childhood dreams come true.

I would like to express my special thanks of gratitude to Amy Gingerich at Herald Press for giving me this golden opportunity to share my stories of my beloved Amish community with the world.

I am overwhelmed with humbleness and thanksgiving to the editors at Herald Press who have helped shape this book into what it is. As I told my editors, I feel as though I'm a plain Jane author that is surrounded by a crew of artists and stylists who have made me feel like a "real" author.

Heartfelt thanks to my Simple Life in New Wilmington Pa Facebook friends who have encouraged, motivated and inspired me to write this book. You have been an amazing support team and I truly feel as though we have become a family.

My sincere thanks to Jim Fisher who has graciously allowed me to share his photographs freely with the world. You are a man of great character and I admire you immensely.

Finally, to my family and friends. Thank you for your loving support and encouragement. I love you deeply.

"Work willingly at whatever you do, as though you were working for the Lord rather than for people. Remember that the Lord will give you an inheritance as your reward, and that the Master you are serving is Christ."
—Colossians 3:23-24 NLT

THE AUTHOR

SUSAN HOUGELMAN is the owner of Western Pennsylvania Hospitality Company and Simple Life Amish Tours. She was born in Pittsburgh but grew up in the Amish countryside of New Wilmington, Pennsylvania, where she has lived and done business with the Amish community for more than twenty years. Through her unique experiences as an Amish tour guide, she has been welcomed into the Old Order Amish community not just as a business acquaintance but also as a trusted friend. Susan has combined her passion for writing, her love for the Lord, and her love for the Amish to create this book of inspirational stories and photographs. Susan is a wife to Joseph, a mother to two daughters, Ally and Lauren, a grandmother to Averie and Alexis, and an English *Mommy* (grandmother) to many Amish children.